The EU Horizons
The Economic Realities Driving Tomorrow's Investments

Exploring the Union's Pathways to
Growth, Resilience, and
Transformation

Bahaa G Arnouk

Bahaa G. Arnouk

Book Cover by Bahaa Arnouk

1st edition 2024

Table of contents

Introduction: Europe's Resilient Tapestry – A Vision of Promise

Welcome to an odyssey across the economic and cultural heartbeat of Europe. In this book, Dr. Arnouk unveils a story far beyond spreadsheets and projections; this is a tale of ambition, transformation, and the indomitable spirit of a continent continually reinventing itself.

Europe is a masterful weaver, threading together centuries of history, boundless innovation, and unyielding resilience. From the sunlit vineyards of France to the cutting-edge tech hubs of Estonia, from Germany's industrial backbone to Spain's sun-drenched fields of renewable energy, every thread tells a story. And when these threads come together, they create a dynamic tapestry—a living, breathing testament to a union that balances its rich heritage with the audacious pursuit of the future.

Dr. Arnouk takes you on a journey that challenges convention and ignites curiosity. With a unique blend of scholarly rigor and storytelling finesse, each chapter explores the economic landscapes that define the European Union. You'll traverse the challenges of green transitions, the pulsating opportunities of digital revolutions, and the heartbeats of nations rebuilding and thriving amid global uncertainty.

Here, the numbers come alive. The GDP figures become more than metrics—they are lifelines of innovation, perseverance, and strategic foresight. Fiscal policies evolve from mundane details into bold strokes of ambition, drawing a roadmap for sustainability and growth. Each nation's narrative is a reminder of Europe's complexity, a mosaic where every piece—large or small—adds vibrancy to the whole.

But this is more than an exploration; it's an invitation. Dr. Arnouk beckons you to see Europe not as a cluster of nations bound by geography but as a bold experiment in unity, resilience, and human ingenuity. This book is a call to envision a continent that is not just surviving but thriving— a beacon of what is possible when diversity meets collaboration and when tradition embraces innovation.

Whether you are an investor seeking new horizons, a policymaker crafting the next chapter of your nation's story, or an intellectually curious reader yearning to understand the forces shaping our world, this book is your gateway. It offers a front-row seat to Europe's journey—a journey where challenges transform into opportunities and where the future is written with the same passion that carved its illustrious past.

So, step into this world shaped by ingenuity and determination. Let Dr. Arnouk guide you through the stories of resilience and the triumph of will. Europe awaits, and its story is yours to discover. Welcome to a journey that promises to inspire, inform, and ignite the possibilities of tomorrow.

Chapter (1)

Germany: A Resilient Economic Hub Facing Complex Challenges and Emerging Opportunities

Germany, located in Central Europe, is the largest economy in the European Union, covering an area of approximately 357,022 square kilometres. As of 2024, its population is estimated to be around 84 million people. Despite experiencing a contraction of 0.2% in GDP in 2023 due to high energy prices and tightening monetary policies, Germany's economy is expected to gradually recover in 2024. The country's GDP is projected to grow by 0.2% in FY24, with a nominal GDP forecast of €4.8 trillion.

Germany, the powerhouse of Europe, finds itself at a critical moment in its economic trajectory. While its reputation for industrial strength and stability remains, the country must navigate significant challenges, from the repercussions of the Russian-Ukrainian conflict to mounting competitive pressures from China. The latest IMF report reveals a nuanced picture of Germany's economic resilience, balanced against substantial demographic, fiscal, and geopolitical challenges. Here's an in-depth look at Germany's economic landscape, where cautious optimism meets potential hurdles, and where savvy investors might find unique opportunities amidst transformation.

A Steady Recovery: Strength and Resilience Amid Global Shifts

Germany's economy is on a path to recovery after weathering recent shocks, including soaring energy costs and global supply chain disruptions exacerbated by the Russian-Ukrainian conflict. Policy adjustments and Germany's robust industrial foundation have helped the country stabilize, with a gradual recovery on the horizon.

Consumer-Driven Growth Prospects: Despite previous economic setbacks, Germany's private consumption is projected to drive economic growth through 2024, as wages outpace inflation. With real wages turning positive, it is anticipated that GDP will grow by 0.2% in 2024 and 1.3% in 2025. Strong wage growth and stable consumption trends provide a promising climate for retail and service investments, even as fiscal and external pressures persist.

Energy Price Stabilization with Geopolitical Underpinnings: Germany's quick pivot away from Russian gas supplies has led to a stabilization of energy prices, reducing inflationary pressures that had previously stifled growth. After the shock of Russian supply disruptions, Germany diversified its energy sources, helping restore wholesale gas prices to manageable levels. It is noticeable that inflation is expected to ease, averaging 2.5% in 2024 and reaching 2.2% by 2025. This shift has major implications for energy-dependent sectors, which can now benefit from a more stable price environment.

Tight Labor Market with Slight Softening Ahead: Germany's unemployment rate, forecast to rise to 3.3% in 2024, reflects a still-tight labor market tempered by modest economic growth projections.

High wage growth has bolstered real household income, supporting consumption, but Germany's rapidly aging workforce signals potential long-term labor supply issues that could impact productivity without proactive policy adjustments in immigration and workforce integration. Germany's resilience in these areas highlights its role as a stable economic leader in Europe, but the economy remains exposed to significant risks, including heightened competition from China and the ongoing ramifications of the Russian-Ukrainian conflict, which has redefined Europe's geopolitical and energy landscape.

Fiscal Realities: Balancing Debt, Demographic Pressures, and Structural Reform

Germany faces multifaceted fiscal challenges, particularly with aging demographics, geopolitical demands, and the green transition driving pressures on public finances. These dynamics demand a balanced approach to reform and investment while ensuring fiscal sustainability.

The Debt Brake and Calls for Fiscal Flexibility: Germany's constitutionally enshrined debt brake has historically provided fiscal stability. However, it is suggested that a moderate easing of the rule could create critical fiscal space for much-needed public investments. Specifically, an adjustment increasing the structural deficit limit by approximately 1% of GDP could enable Germany to meet rising demands in infrastructure, digitalization, and green energy initiatives. This adjustment would still ensure debt sustainability, particularly given Germany's low public debt-to-GDP ratio relative to other advanced economies. The current adherence to the debt brake necessitates a rapid pace of debt reduction, potentially limiting fiscal flexibility in critical investment areas like transportation, energy, and digital infrastructure.

Addressing Rising Spending Pressures: Germany's fiscal challenges are compounded by aging-related costs and defence spending. Over the medium term, public pension and healthcare costs are projected to increase by 0.9% and 0.7% of GDP, respectively, necessitating federal transfers to sustain the pension system. Concurrently, rising defence expenditures, partially funded by a special fund set to expire in 2027, highlight the need for sustainable financing mechanisms. Addressing these pressures, alongside green transition investments, would require additional annual expenditures of at least 1.2% of GDP.

Revenue and Expenditure Reforms: Germany could explore a combination of revenue-enhancing and cost-saving measures to bolster fiscal capacity. Reducing environmentally harmful subsidies, which currently amount to 0.4% of GDP, and increasing taxation on real estate and goods. Realigning inheritance tax policies and closing loopholes could also contribute to fiscal consolidation. On the expenditure side, aligning pension increases with inflation rather than wage growth and linking retirement ages to life expectancy could alleviate long-term fiscal pressures. Germany's current practice of underspending allocated investment budgets further underscores the need for improved execution in public investment planning and procurement processes.

Structural Reforms and Policy Implementation

Structural reforms are critical for Germany to address both immediate challenges and the country's long-term economic trajectory. These reforms aim to mitigate labor shortages, enhance productivity, and ensure Germany remains competitive while addressing pressing demographic and environmental challenges. Key measures include:

Addressing Labor Shortages:

Expanding Access to Childcare and Eldercare Services: To integrate more individuals, particularly women, into the full-time labor market, Germany must enhance access to affordable and reliable childcare and eldercare services. These measures would reduce the opportunity cost of work, especially for women, who often take on caregiving responsibilities. Expanding these services is crucial for boosting labor force participation rates and addressing Germany's aging workforce.

Reducing Marginal Tax Rates for Second Earners: High marginal tax rates for second earners in married households discourage full-time work. Policy changes to reduce these disincentives, making full-time employment more financially viable for secondary earners, particularly women. This reform is expected to not only boost household incomes but also alleviate labor market tightness.

Increasing Integration of Immigrants: Immigration has historically supported Germany's workforce, but there is a need for better integration measures. This includes language training, recognition of foreign qualifications, and support for job placement to ensure immigrants can contribute effectively to the economy.

Enhancing Productivity and Innovation:

Cutting Red Tape: Simplifying bureaucratic processes is critical to fostering entrepreneurship and supporting businesses, particularly small and medium enterprises (SMEs). Streamlined regulatory processes can accelerate the deployment of renewable energy projects, infrastructure investments, and other critical growth-enhancing initiatives.

Fostering Innovation through Digitalization: Germany must accelerate the expansion of its digital infrastructure, particularly fiber-optic networks, to remain competitive in the global digital economy. Institutional investments in venture capital should be encouraged to support startups and technological innovation. Additionally, reducing barriers to the adoption of digital solutions by businesses would bolster productivity.

Deepening the European Single Market: Progressing toward a European Capital Markets Union and harmonizing regulations across the EU would provide German firms with greater access to funding and facilitate cross-border investment. This reform would enhance Germany's position as a hub for trade and innovation within the EU.

Streamlining Energy and Climate Policies

Renewable Energy Projects: While Germany has made progress in expediting approvals for renewable energy projects, further streamlining is necessary to meet its ambitious climate targets. Removing administrative barriers and providing clear guidelines to accelerate the deployment of solar and wind energy infrastructure.

Green Transition Investments: Substantial investment is required to upgrade transportation, energy, and digital infrastructure to support the green transition. Germany must align its industrial and climate policies to ensure resources are directed toward sustainable growth initiatives.

Adapting to Demographic Shifts

Life Expectancy-Linked Retirement Age: To address the fiscal strain of an aging population, Germany should consider linking retirement ages to life expectancy. This measure would help stabilize pension systems and ensure a sustainable labor force over the long term.

Upskilling the Workforce: Providing reskilling and upskilling opportunities for workers is essential for adapting to the demands of a transitioning economy. Targeted training programs in high-demand fields, such as green energy, digital technologies, and advanced manufacturing, will ensure a smooth transition for workers displaced by automation and structural changes.

Balancing Immediate Demands and Long-Term Sustainability: Recalibrating Germany's fiscal and structural policies to balance short-term economic recovery with long-term resilience is urgent. Investing in future-oriented sectors, addressing demographic shifts, and modernizing fiscal and structural frameworks will be critical in ensuring Germany remains competitive and sustainable in an increasingly volatile global landscape. By implementing these reforms, Germany can bolster its economic foundation, address labor market challenges, and secure a leadership role in driving Europe's green and digital transitions.

Investment Horizons: Promising Sectors Amid Transformative Shifts

Despite fiscal constraints, Germany's investment landscape is rich with sectors aligned with policy priorities and growth potential. Key sectors positioned to thrive in Germany's economy, even as global competition and demographic changes shape the investment horizon.

Renewable Energy and Sustainability Initiatives:

Germany remains at the forefront of global climate action, leveraging its commitment to achieving ambitious decarbonization goals. It is noteworthy to mention that

Germany's response to the energy crisis precipitated by the Russian-Ukrainian conflict, which catalyzed significant progress in renewable energy development:

Streamlined Approvals for Renewable Projects: Germany has prioritized accelerating approval processes for solar and wind energy projects, a critical step toward meeting its climate targets. This focus is evidenced by the removal of bureaucratic bottlenecks that have traditionally delayed infrastructure projects.

Offshore Wind Energy Expansion: Recent commitments include substantial investments in offshore wind farms, targeting significant capacity increases by 2030. These initiatives not only enhance energy security but also provide lucrative opportunities for investors in renewable energy infrastructure.

Hydrogen Economy Development: Germany is scaling up investments in green hydrogen technologies as part of its energy transition strategy. Projects focused on hydrogen production, storage, and distribution are positioned to attract substantial private and public funding.

For investors, Germany's renewable energy initiatives offer a stable and policy-aligned sector, further supported by government incentives and a clear regulatory framework.

Technology and Digital Innovation

Germany's digital transformation agenda underscores significant investments in infrastructure and innovation to bolster its competitiveness in an increasingly tech-driven global economy:

Expansion of Fibre-Optic Networks: The government has allocated significant resources to expand fibre-optic connectivity, addressing a historical lag in digital infrastructure. This initiative aims to connect underserved regions, thereby enabling broader participation in the digital economy.

AI and Cloud Computing Investments: Germany's strategic focus on AI and cloud technologies includes targeted investments to develop domestic capabilities and reduce reliance on foreign providers. Public-private partnerships in these fields are growing, offering robust opportunities for innovation-driven investors.

Support for Startups and Venture Capital: The government's efforts to promote venture capital funding for startups in high-tech sectors. These measures aim to create a dynamic ecosystem fostering entrepreneurship and technological breakthroughs.

With growing global competition, particularly from China, Germany's push to solidify its digital economy presents not just a defensive strategy but a lucrative investment frontier.

Healthcare and Aging Economy

Germany's aging population presents both challenges and investment opportunities, as highlighted in the IMF's projections of rising healthcare expenditures:

Growth in Healthcare Technology and Biotech: Rising demand for advanced healthcare services has spurred innovation in medical devices, diagnostics, and biopharmaceuticals. Companies operating in these fields are likely to benefit from increased public and private investments.

Expansion of Eldercare Infrastructure: Investments in eldercare facilities and technologies, such as smart home solutions tailored for senior living, are gaining momentum. Public funding for eldercare services is expected to grow, driven by demographic realities.

Focus on Efficiency through Digital Health: Germany is also investing in telemedicine and digital health platforms to enhance healthcare delivery and reduce system inefficiencies. This trend aligns with global shifts toward integrating technology into healthcare services.

These trends position the healthcare sector as a stable and expanding investment domain in the German economy.

Manufacturing and Export Excellence in the Face of Global Competition

Germany's manufacturing sector, a cornerstone of its economic strength, is undergoing transformation to adapt to shifting global trade dynamics:

Focus on High-Value Products: Germany is transitioning toward high-value-added manufacturing, emphasizing sectors like advanced machinery, automotive innovation (including electric vehicles), and industrial robotics. These shifts respond to rising competition from China and other emerging markets.

Resilience in Export Markets: Germany continues to maintain a strong trade surplus, supported by its competitive manufacturing exports. Efforts to diversify export markets, particularly in light of geopolitical uncertainties, provide a buffer against potential trade disruptions.

Sustainability in Manufacturing: Investments in green manufacturing technologies, such as carbon-neutral production processes, align with Germany's environmental goals and enhance its attractiveness to sustainability-conscious investors.

These adaptations ensure that Germany's manufacturing sector remains a reliable yet innovative investment area.

Strategic Initiatives Supporting Investment Growth:

Germany's investment strategy is not limited to individual sectors but is integrated into broader economic policies:

Public-Private Collaboration: Programs like the Generationenkapital, which involves the strategic investment of federal funds to support public pensions, underscore Germany's commitment to leveraging financial markets for long-term growth.

Enhanced Investment Execution: Germany is addressing its historical challenges with underspending allocated budgets by improving public investment planning and procurement processes. These reforms aim to ensure that funds earmarked for infrastructure and innovation are fully utilized.

Germany's investment landscape is shaped by its proactive response to global challenges and its alignment with future-oriented policies. The sectors of energy, digital technology, healthcare, and manufacturing—are central to Germany's strategy for sustainable growth and resilience, offering a wide array of opportunities for investors.

Takeaways for Investors: Balancing Opportunity and Risk

Germany's investment landscape presents a mix of growth potential and fiscal caution, requiring a thoughtful investment approach. Here are some strategies for navigating Germany's economic landscape:

Align with Policy and ESG Priorities: The German government's focus on renewable energy, digital transformation, and healthcare aligns with EU policy priorities. Investors can leverage these sectors, which are likely to benefit from sustained government support and regulatory stability.

Sector-Specific Caution Amid Global Pressures: There are potential risks within Germany's real estate market, particularly commercial real estate (CRE), where prices have dropped due to high interest rates and changing market demands. Investors should be cautious about CRE exposure and consider sectors with stronger fundamentals, such as technology and healthcare.

Sustainability and Long-Term Focus: ESG-focused investors can capitalize on Germany's strong commitment to sustainable practices. With established government support for green industries, Germany's sustainable sectors offer a long-term growth outlook that aligns with both environmental goals and regulatory frameworks.

Diverse Portfolios for Resilience: While Germany's market remains stable, the demographic pressures and geopolitical risks could impact growth. Diversifying across sectors—such as technology, renewable energy, healthcare, and high-value manufacturing—can help mitigate these risks, enabling investors to capture growth while managing volatility.

Germany's Future Path: Resilience in an Evolving Global Landscape

Germany's economic outlook remains robust, underpinned by strategic sectors that align with global priorities. However, fiscal challenges, demographic shifts, and heightened competition—particularly from China—add complexity to the nation's growth trajectory. Investors with a long-term, balanced approach can find ample opportunities in Germany's diverse economic landscape, but success will require navigating the nuanced risks posed by fiscal pressures, global competition, and the ongoing impacts of the Russian Ukrainian conflict. For those prepared to invest with a strategic vision, Germany offers a blend of stability, innovation, and sustainable growth.

Chapter (2)

France: A Resilient Economy in Transition Amid Growing Fiscal Pressures and Green Ambitions

France, located in Western Europe, spans an area of approximately 551,695 square kilometres. It is home to around 67 million people in 2024. The French economy has remained resilient despite challenges like the pandemic and the energy crisis, with real GDP growth projected to be 0.9% in FY24. France's nominal GDP is expected to reach approximately €2.9 trillion, while inflation is forecast to decline to 2.3% in 2024.

As the second-largest economy in the Eurozone, France faces a complex economic landscape shaped by recent global shocks and its ambitious green and digital transformation agendas. While its economic recovery has shown signs of resilience, the country grapples with fiscal pressures, an aging population, and geopolitical challenges. The latest IMF consultation report offers valuable insights into France's economic outlook, detailing its ongoing recovery, fiscal consolidation efforts, and the significant opportunities for growth in critical sectors. Below is an in-depth exploration of France's economic environment, highlighting key trends and areas where investors may find promising opportunities.

Economic Recovery: Gradual Growth Amidst Global Challenges

France's economy has displayed resilience in the face of multiple shocks, including the COVID-19 pandemic and the energy crisis triggered by the Russian invasion of Ukraine. Despite a slowdown in 2023, GDP grew by 1.1%, supported by net exports, especially in aeronautics and textiles. However, domestic demand remained weak, and investment, particularly in residential construction, surprised on the downside.

Moderate Growth in 2024: France's economy is projected to grow by 0.9% in 2024, driven by recovery in exports and a gradual pickup in investment. While inflation pressures have eased significantly since 2023, the path to a full recovery remains uncertain, with global factors, such as geopolitical tensions and a potential slowdown in major trading partners, influencing the outlook.

Disinflationary Progress: Inflation, which peaked at 7.3% in early 2023, is on track to fall to 2.3% by the end of 2024, thanks to easing energy prices and improved supply chain conditions. Core inflation, which excludes volatile food and energy prices, is also declining, albeit at a slower pace, highlighting ongoing challenges in the services sector.

Labor Market Strength: France's labor market remains robust, with low unemployment rates around 7.4% in 2024, despite weaker economic conditions. However, labor productivity has yet to recover fully from the pandemic-induced disruptions, and structural reforms in the pension and unemployment systems are expected to support longer-term job growth and productivity improvement.

Fiscal Strategy: Navigating High Debt and Demographic Pressures

Fiscal consolidation is critical as France seeks to reduce its public debt and meet rising demands for investment in green and digital initiatives. The fiscal deficit reached 5.5% of GDP in 2023, driven by underperformance in tax revenues and higher-than-expected spending. The 2024 budget aims to reduce the deficit to 5.1%, but the road to fiscal sustainability is steep.

Pension and Unemployment Benefit Reforms: Reforms to the pension system and unemployment benefits are yielding positive outcomes, including reductions in structural unemployment and improved labor force participation rates, particularly among women. These reforms are projected to raise potential output by 0.5% by 2028. However, additional measures are required to address underlying inefficiencies and fully achieve the deficit reduction target of below 3% of GDP by 2027.

Public Debt Concerns: With public debt projected at 111.3% of GDP in 2024 and set to rise without substantial fiscal adjustments, managing debt sustainability is an urgent priority. Well-specified package of fiscal consolidation measures, focusing on rationalizing current spending while safeguarding investments in critical areas like green energy and digital infrastructure is essential. Political uncertainties and rising interest rates could exacerbate debt pressures, emphasizing the need for swift and targeted action.

Tax and Spending Reforms: The French government has initiated broad-based spending reviews, identifying areas such as health, education, and social security for efficiency gains. The ongoing efforts to streamline public expenditures include reducing overlaps across governmental levels, optimizing the public sector wage bill, and leveraging digital solutions to improve service delivery. Additionally, tax expenditures are being reassessed to enhance economic efficiency and reduce fiscal costs. These measures aim to align fiscal policies with long-term growth objectives while preparing for challenges posed by demographic shifts and climate transitions.

Medium-Term Fiscal Outlook: Under current policies, the deficit will remain elevated at 4.5% of GDP by 2027, well above the 3% Maastricht limit. Bringing the deficit below 3% of GDP by 2027 would require a substantial structural primary effort averaging almost 1% of GDP annually over 2025–2027. This adjustment is critical to placing France's public debt on a downward trajectory and ensuring fiscal resilience. The government's commitment to fiscal prudence, complemented by targeted measures like tighter eligibility for unemployment benefits and enhanced local government spending oversight, will be crucial for long-term fiscal health.

The combination of structural reforms and prudent fiscal management provides a pathway to address France's fiscal challenges while enabling strategic investments in areas critical for future competitiveness and resilience.

Investment Horizons: Green Transition, Digital Innovation, and More

Despite fiscal constraints, France's transformation towards a greener and more digital economy presents significant investment opportunities. Government-led initiatives and targeted spending in strategic areas aim to bolster long-term growth while addressing global challenges like climate change, digital competitiveness, and supply chain resilience.

Green Economy and Renewable Energy

France's green transition lies at the core of its economic agenda, with a robust focus on achieving net-zero greenhouse gas emissions. The government has prioritized the following projects and policies:

Building Renovations: Significant funding is directed toward energy efficiency upgrades in residential and public buildings. These efforts are expected to reduce carbon emissions while creating job opportunities in construction and retrofitting sectors.

Public Transport Expansion: Investments in low-emission public transport, such as high-speed rail and urban transit systems, are accelerating, supporting sustainable mobility and reducing reliance on fossil fuels.

Low-Emission Vehicles: Incentives for the adoption of electric and hybrid vehicles are coupled with expanding charging infrastructure across the country, positioning France as a key player in the automotive green transformation.

Renewable Energy Projects: France is scaling up solar and wind energy capacity, with offshore wind projects, in particular, gaining traction. These initiatives aim to diversify the energy mix, enhance energy security, and reduce dependence on imported fossil fuels.

These initiatives are crucial to meeting France's long-term climate commitments and supporting its competitive edge in the global green economy.

Digital Transformation

France is rapidly advancing its digital capabilities, leveraging public and private investments to drive innovation and economic growth. Key projects and initiatives include:

Fibre Optic Expansion: To close the digital divide, France is accelerating the deployment of fibre-optic networks nationwide. This project aims to ensure high-speed internet access for households and businesses, particularly in rural areas, fostering economic inclusion.

Artificial Intelligence (AI) and Cloud Computing: The government has allocated funding to support the development of AI applications and the establishment of secure cloud infrastructure. These efforts aim to solidify France's position as a leader in cutting-edge digital technologies.

Digital Education and Workforce Training: Significant resources are being channeled into training programs to upskill the workforce in digital competencies. These initiatives align with the broader EU goals of enhancing digital literacy and competitiveness.

Support for Startups and Tech Ecosystems: France's "French Tech" initiative continues to provide funding and regulatory support to emerging tech companies, fostering a thriving startup ecosystem. These efforts are expected to enhance innovation and attract international investment.

Manufacturing and Export Growth

Manufacturing remains a cornerstone of France's economy, supported by government initiatives to enhance competitiveness and adapt to global trade shifts. Key highlights include:

Aeronautics Leadership: France's aeronautics sector is recovering strongly, with exports driven by robust demand for aircraft and advanced engineering solutions. Continued innovation in green aviation technologies offers substantial growth opportunities.

Automotive Industry Transformation: Investments in electric vehicle (EV) production and associated supply chains, such as battery manufacturing, are strengthening France's position in the global automotive market.

Advanced Manufacturing and Reshoring Initiatives: The government's focus on reshoring critical industries and modernizing production facilities supports manufacturing resilience while reducing dependency on volatile global supply chains.

Export-Driven Growth: Strategic sectors like capital goods and textiles are benefiting from France's export recovery, with tourism and financial services also contributing positively to the trade balance.

These targeted investments underscore France's commitment to fostering a sustainable and digitally competitive economy while preserving its manufacturing legacy. These strategic sectors not only drive growth but also present opportunities for domestic and international investors seeking alignment with France's transformation agenda.

Risks and Opportunities: Balancing Economic Challenges with Growth Potential

While France's economic outlook is positive, the road ahead is fraught with risks, particularly in the areas of fiscal sustainability, demographic shifts, and geopolitical tensions.

Political Fragmentation and Fiscal Uncertainty

Domestic political fragmentation and policy uncertainty could delay necessary fiscal reforms, affecting investor confidence and economic growth. The outcome of France's 2024 legislative elections with a New Popular Front (NFP) in the lower house of parliament, a left-wing alliance that won 182 seats, a centrist coalition with only 168 seats and a hard-wing party that won only 143 seats, the NFP is short of majority and the country has got a hung parliament that is shaping the country's fiscal and economic trajectory.

Risks of delayed fiscal consolidation due to political impasses
are anticipated, which could weigh on investor confidence
and slow economic recovery. Without decisive policy action,
France's deficit could remain elevated, straining its ability to
meet the Maastricht deficit limit of 3% of GDP by 2027.
Furthermore, prolonged fiscal uncertainty could exacerbate
borrowing costs, as sovereign bond spreads are sensitive to
political developments.

Nevertheless, political fragmentation also opens a window
for consensus-building across parties to prioritize structural
reforms, particularly those aimed at reducing inefficiencies in
public spending and addressing long-term fiscal
sustainability. Well-structured agreements could unlock new
fiscal pathways to support growth-friendly investments in
green and digital transitions.

Geopolitical and Global Economic Risks

France faces significant external risks stemming from
geopolitical instability and uncertainties in global economic
growth. The ongoing war in Ukraine continues to disrupt
European energy markets and supply chains, with knock-on
effects on French industries reliant on stable global trade
conditions. This is particularly concerning for sectors such as
aeronautics, automotive, and capital goods, which are
sensitive to shifts in external demand.

Geopolitical tensions and potential escalations in trade
protectionism could pose additional challenges. A slowdown
in major trading partners, particularly within the Eurozone,
would dampen export growth and hinder France's post-

pandemic recovery trajectory. Tourism, a key driver of services exports, also remains vulnerable to global economic uncertainties and consumer sentiment.

Despite these risks, France's strong focus on diversifying trade partnerships and enhancing competitiveness in green and digital technologies provides a robust counterbalance. Initiatives to reduce dependency on volatile supply chains and to strengthen domestic production capacity, particularly in energy and critical industries, align with the government's broader resilience strategy.

Opportunities Amidst Challenges

While risks are pronounced, opportunities exist to pivot challenges into growth drivers:

Resilient Fiscal Strategies: By leveraging spending reviews and targeting fiscal inefficiencies, France can optimize resources for strategic investments, bolstering both short-term recovery and long-term competitiveness.

Geopolitical Cooperation: France's leadership in multilateral cooperation within the European Union and its commitment to climate and digital transitions position it as a key player in addressing global challenges collaboratively.

Innovation-Driven Growth: Investments in cutting-edge sectors, such as renewable energy, AI, and advanced manufacturing, can mitigate some external risks by fostering a competitive edge in the global market.

France's ability to navigate these interconnected risks while capitalizing on its strengths will be critical in shaping its economic trajectory over the medium term. For investors, the evolving landscape demands cautious optimism, with a focus on sectors aligned with France's resilience and growth strategies.

Strategic Takeaways for Investors:

France's evolving economic landscape, shaped by fiscal reforms, green and digital transitions, and global uncertainties, presents both risks and opportunities for investors. Strategic focus on high-potential sectors and alignment with government priorities will be crucial for long-term success.

Focus on Green and Digital Sectors

France's ambitious goals in renewable energy, digital transformation, and sustainable technologies offer significant growth opportunities. The government's robust backing of these sectors, demonstrated through targeted investments and policy incentives, creates a favorable environment for innovation and expansion. Key areas for investor focus include:

Renewable Energy: France is ramping up investments in offshore wind projects and solar energy expansion, supported by incentives to diversify its energy mix. Additionally, energy efficiency programs in building renovations and industrial processes align with its commitment to reduce carbon emissions and dependency on imported fossil fuels.

Digital Infrastructure: Public and private investments in digital infrastructure, such as nationwide fibre-optic rollout and cloud computing, are key enablers of economic modernization. Furthermore, the government's support for AI development and cybersecurity enhancements opens opportunities in the tech sector.

Sustainable Transportation: Investments in electric vehicle (EV) infrastructure, including charging networks and zero-emission public transit, reflect France's commitment to sustainable mobility. These initiatives are creating avenues for growth in the automotive and transport industries, particularly for companies developing innovative green solutions.

By aligning investments with France's priorities in these areas, investors can tap into government-supported growth engines that are resilient to broader economic pressures.

Monitor Fiscal Developments

France's fiscal strategy involves striking a balance between reducing deficits and fostering economic growth. While the government prioritizes targeted spending in green and digital transitions, it is also conducting spending reviews to address inefficiencies in sectors like healthcare, education, and social security. These fiscal adjustments create both opportunities and risks for investors:

Opportunities in Priority Sectors: Sectors aligned with government priorities, such as green infrastructure, defense, and digital education, are likely to receive continued support and funding despite fiscal constraints. Investments in these areas could benefit from long-term policy stability.

Caution in Tax-Sensitive Industries: Industries sensitive to potential tax hikes or reductions in public spending—such as luxury goods, non-essential services, or energy-intensive manufacturing—require careful consideration. Risks associated with fiscal uncertainty, including possible policy delays due to political fragmentation, could affect market confidence.

Debt and Interest Rate Risks: As France seeks to reduce its high public debt, investors should monitor interest rate developments and their impact on sectors reliant on government borrowing or consumer spending. Sovereign debt risks, while assessed as moderate by the IMF, could lead to volatility in bond markets, indirectly affecting broader investment landscapes.

Diversify Investments

Given the multifaceted risks stemming from fiscal adjustments, political fragmentation, and global geopolitical tensions, diversification remains a prudent investment strategy. Key diversification opportunities include:

Technology and Digital Innovation: France's robust tech ecosystem, driven by initiatives like "French Tech," offers growth opportunities in startups, AI, and digital services. These sectors are relatively insulated from fiscal tightening and benefit from government support.

Healthcare: The healthcare sector, identified as a critical area for spending reviews, offers potential for efficiency-driven growth. Digital health solutions, biotechnology, and pharmaceutical advancements align with France's strategic goals of modernizing public services.

Advanced Manufacturing and Exports: Manufacturing sectors like aeronautics and automotive are poised for recovery, supported by export growth and innovation in green and digital technologies. Investments in these industries can balance exposure to domestic economic risks with global market opportunities.

Long-Term Outlook

France's medium-term growth outlook depends on the success of its structural reforms and fiscal consolidation efforts. Investors who align their strategies with these macroeconomic trends—while diversifying to mitigate risks—stand to benefit from the country's transformation into a green and digital economy.

By adopting a targeted yet flexible approach, investors can navigate France's fiscal and geopolitical uncertainties while positioning themselves to capture the growth opportunities inherent in its strategic priorities.

A Balanced Path Forward for France's Economic Transformation

France stands at a pivotal juncture as it navigates a complex economic landscape defined by fiscal challenges, demographic pressures, and the imperative for green and digital transformation. The resilience demonstrated by its economy in the face of global shocks, coupled with strategic investments in key sectors, underscores its potential for sustainable growth.

The government's commitment to fiscal consolidation, while addressing inefficiencies in public spending, lays the groundwork for a more stable economic environment. Structural reforms in pensions, unemployment benefits, and taxation, alongside targeted spending in green energy and digital infrastructure, exemplify France's dual focus on economic modernization and fiscal prudence. However, political fragmentation and global uncertainties present tangible risks that must be carefully managed to ensure the success of these reforms.

France's ambitious agenda for green transition and digital innovation positions it as a leader in sectors critical to the future global economy. The drive to expand renewable energy, bolster digital capabilities, and revitalize manufacturing creates significant opportunities for investors, especially those aligned with sustainable and innovative growth trajectories. At the same time, the country's focus on reshoring industries and enhancing resilience in critical supply chains reflects a proactive response to the challenges of geopolitical and economic volatility.

For investors, France presents a landscape of both opportunity and caution. The need for fiscal discipline and potential shifts in policy due to political dynamics require careful monitoring. Diversified investment strategies that prioritize high-growth sectors like technology, healthcare, and advanced manufacturing can help mitigate risks while capturing long-term value.

Ultimately, France's ability to balance fiscal sustainability with strategic investments in green and digital transitions will determine its economic trajectory. As the country adapts to its evolving challenges and opportunities, it remains a key player in the Eurozone, offering robust potential for growth and innovation in an uncertain global environment. For those prepared to navigate its complexities, France offers a compelling narrative of resilience and transformation.

Chapter (3)

Italy: A Resilient Economy with Strong Investment Potential Despite Structural Challenges

Italy, located in Southern Europe, covers an area of approximately 301,340 square kilometres and has a population of around 60.4 million people in 2024. The country's economy has demonstrated resilience, with real GDP growth projected at 0.7% in FY24. Italy's nominal GDP for the year is estimated to reach approximately €2.1 trillion.

Italy's economic outlook in 2024 is marked by cautious optimism, underscored by a recovery from the COVID-19 and energy price shocks. While growth in 202 3 was moderate at 0.9%, Italy's economy is projected to stabilize with gradual improvements. Despite challenges such as weak productivity, an aging population, and ongoing fiscal pressures, Italy presents an investment environment rich with opportunities—especially in the green and digital transitions, infrastructure development, and private sector innovation. The IMF's recent consultation report highlights Italy's strengths and risks, offering a roadmap for future growth and investment.

Economic Outlook: Growth Moderates but Resilience Remains

Italy's real GDP increased by 0.9% in 2023, a significant milestone as it exceeded pre-pandemic levels for the first time in 15 years. Growth is forecast to moderate in the coming years, stabilizing at around 0.7% in 2024. However, the recovery remains robust compared to other Eurozone economies. Key growth drivers have included private consumption and investment, supported by tax incentives such as the Super-bonus for home renovations and credits for capital equipment purchases. The National Recovery and Resilience Plan (NRRP), financed through EU funds, has further contributed to the economic rebound. Despite these positive developments, long-term challenges such as a shrinking workforce and persistent low productivity growth continue to weigh on the country's outlook.

Private Consumption and Investment

Private consumption has benefited from strong job growth, declining household saving rates, and targeted tax and social security reductions that have increased disposable income. Investment activity, while bolstered by tax credits and public spending under the NRRP, has not yet fully rebounded to pre-pandemic levels. Residential investments, driven by the Superbonus, have started to taper off, but increased spending on non-residential construction and capital equipment has partially offset this decline.

Private sector investment in sustaining future growth, particularly in productivity-enhancing sectors such as technology and infrastructure is paramount. Successful implementation of NRRP reforms and investments is expected to play a pivotal role in revitalizing private investment. However, delays in NRRP execution or reforms could hinder this progress.

Labor Market

The labor market has shown significant improvement, with the unemployment rate declining to 7.7% in 2023 and the employment rate reaching a record high of 62.25%. Employment growth has been driven by labor-intensive sectors such as services, tourism, and construction, with the latter boosted by fiscal incentives and NRRP projects. However, skill shortages remain a critical challenge, with 45% of businesses reporting hiring difficulties due to a mismatch between labor market needs and available skills.

Demographic factors further exacerbate labor market pressures. Italy's working-age population continues to decline, driven by low fertility rates and an aging population. Female labor force participation, while improving, remains below EU averages, limiting the country's labor market potential. To address these challenges, Italy is focusing on policies aimed at increasing labor force participation among women and older workers. Work-life balance initiatives, expanded childcare support, and vocational training programs are expected to boost labor force engagement in the medium term. Additionally, plans to issue permits for 450,000 non-EU workers in the coming years aim to alleviate immediate labor shortages.

Long-Term Challenges

Despite near-term resilience, Italy faces structural challenges, including low productivity growth and a high public debt burden. Labor productivity has stagnated over the past two decades, reflecting inefficiencies in key sectors and a lack of innovation-driven growth. Structural reforms to improve business competitiveness and educational outcomes is vital, which are critical for addressing these issues.

The demographic decline further complicates Italy's economic outlook. Policies to encourage higher fertility rates, coupled with efforts to improve the compatibility of work and family life, are essential for reversing long-term labor force decline. Without these measures, demographic pressures will likely weigh on potential growth over the coming decades.

Inflation and Price Stability: Heading Toward Target

Italy has experienced a significant decline in inflation, with headline inflation dropping to 0.9% in June 2024, marking a rapid and orderly disinflationary process. This reduction has been largely driven by a sharp decrease in energy prices, which had previously been a significant contributor to inflationary pressures. Core inflation, which excludes volatile components such as energy and unprocessed food, has also moderated, reaching 2.1% year-on-year by mid-2024. This moderation in core inflation signals an environment of improving price stability in the near term.

Inflation is projected to stabilize at approximately 2% by 2025, aligning with the European Central Bank's (ECB) medium-term target. This trajectory reflects expectations of continued disinflation in energy prices and contained growth in other cost pressures, including wages. The gradual normalization of inflation is expected to support household purchasing power and maintain real income gains, aiding broader economic stability.

Drivers of Disinflation

The recent decline in inflation has been primarily driven by a combination of global and domestic factors:

Energy Prices: Energy deflation has played a pivotal role, reflecting easing pressures in global commodity markets and improved energy security within Italy. Gas supplies, which had previously been disrupted, have stabilized, reducing costs for households and businesses.

Supply Chains: The normalization of global supply chains has alleviated cost pressures in key manufacturing and distribution sectors. This has helped stabilize prices for goods and services.

Moderated Profit Margins: After a period of elevated unit profit margins, businesses have begun to absorb input cost fluctuations, reducing their impact on consumer prices.

Risks to Price Stability

While inflation is projected to remain near the ECB's target, several risks could disrupt this outlook:

Wage Growth Outpacing Productivity: If wage increases significantly exceed productivity gains, unit labor costs could rise, exerting upward pressure on prices. While recent wage agreements have remained moderate, continued vigilance is needed to ensure wage growth aligns with productivity improvements.

Energy Market Volatility: Unexpected increases in energy prices, whether due to geopolitical tensions or supply disruptions, could reignite inflationary pressures. Italy's reliance on imported energy, despite recent diversification efforts, leaves it exposed to external shocks.

Supply Chain Fragility: Although global supply chains have improved, renewed disruptions or geoeconomic fragmentation could lead to higher import prices, impacting consumer goods.

Policy Implications and the Role of the ECB

Maintaining a balanced monetary policy stance to support price stability is critical. The ECB's efforts to ensure monetary transmission across Eurozone economies have been effective, with interest rate adjustments contributing to the moderation in inflation without significantly stifling economic growth. Italy's inflation trajectory benefits from the ECB's proactive policy measures and its commitment to maintaining price stability.

At the national level, that fiscal policies should complement monetary efforts by avoiding inflationary spending and focusing on structural reforms that boost productivity and competitiveness. Enhanced coordination between fiscal and monetary policies will be essential in navigating potential shocks and maintaining inflation within target levels.

Looking ahead, it is projected that inflation to remain subdued, underscoring an environment conducive to economic stability. This aligns with broader expectations of a steady monetary policy approach and further easing of energy and commodity prices. However, continued attention to productivity growth, wage dynamics, and external risks will be crucial to ensuring inflation remains anchored at sustainable levels.

Fiscal Policy: Navigating Debt Sustainability and Reforms

Italy's fiscal policy remains focused on managing its elevated public debt, which, although reduced from its peak of 155% of GDP in 2020, continues to pose significant long-term risks. As of 2023, the public debt-to-GDP ratio had declined to 137.3%, supported by strong nominal GDP growth and delayed recognition of incurred tax credit liabilities. However, the debt ratio is projected to resume an upward trajectory from 2024 due to latent fiscal pressures and structural inefficiencies. Achieving sustainable debt reduction will require a more aggressive fiscal consolidation strategy, a primary surplus of 3% of GDP by 2025-2026 to stabilize and gradually reduce debt levels is inevitably recommended.

Key Fiscal Reforms

To achieve debt sustainability, Italy must implement critical fiscal reforms that focus on both revenue enhancement and expenditure efficiency:

Narrowing Tax Exemptions: The tax system, while generating high revenue relative to GDP, is burdened by significant inefficiencies, including widespread exemptions and preferential treatments. Rationalizing tax expenditures, which cost approximately 6-7% of GDP annually, would broaden the tax base, increase progressivity, and enhance fiscal stability. Updating real estate valuations in the cadastre, which have not been revised since the 1980s, and expanding property taxes to primary residences are among the measures suggested to address fiscal imbalances.

Reducing Inefficient Spending: High public spending, particularly on pensions and other age-related expenditures, continues to strain fiscal resources. There is an essential need to control pension spending pressures through measures such as raising the effective retirement age, phasing out actuarially costly early retirement schemes, and better targeting pension supplements to those in need.

Scaling Back Public Guarantees: Italy's stock of publicly guaranteed loans, which surged during the COVID-19 crisis, remains high. Gradual reduction of these guarantees, particularly those issued during the pandemic, will help limit contingent liabilities and create fiscal space for growth-enhancing investments.

Challenges in Fiscal Consolidation

Italy's efforts to achieve fiscal consolidation face several structural and cyclical challenges:

Expenditure Pressures: Rising costs associated with pensions, long-term care, and healthcare—driven by an aging population—are projected to significantly increase public spending over the next decade. Pension expenditures alone are expected to rise by 2 percentage points of GDP, peaking in the late 2030s before declining.

Limited Fiscal Space: While nominal GDP growth and improvements in tax compliance have provided temporary relief, Italy's fiscal space remains constrained by its high debt burden and ongoing spending commitments. Current fiscal deficits, which remain above pre-pandemic levels, necessitate urgent measures to align fiscal policies with sustainability goals.

Structural Reforms: Beyond short-term adjustments, deeper structural reforms are needed to address underlying inefficiencies in Italy's fiscal framework. These include enhancing public sector efficiency, streamlining governance over tax credits, and introducing a robust medium-term budgetary framework to improve fiscal planning and control.

Policy Recommendations

To mitigate risks and strengthen fiscal sustainability, the following policy enhancements are recommended:

Frontloaded Fiscal Adjustment: A decisive fiscal adjustment strategy, implemented over the next two to three years, would help Italy achieve the recommended primary surplus target. This includes phasing out temporary measures, such as housing renovation grants, and using revenue overperformance to reduce debt rather than increase spending.

Productivity-Enhancing Investments: Fiscal resources should be redirected toward high-multiplier investments in infrastructure, education, and digital transitions. These investments, supported by the National Recovery and Resilience Plan (NRRP), can drive long-term growth while maintaining fiscal discipline.

Improved Oversight of Tax Credits: Strengthening oversight of tax credit programs, including the newly introduced incentives for green and digital investments, will reduce fiscal risks. Real-time monitoring and compliance mechanisms are critical to ensuring these programs achieve their intended economic benefits without undermining fiscal targets.

While Italy has demonstrated resilience in navigating fiscal challenges, achieving long-term debt sustainability will require bold policy measures and unwavering commitment to reform. Timely and effective implementation of fiscal consolidation measures, coupled with structural reforms to enhance productivity, will be crucial in addressing the twin challenges of high debt and limited fiscal space. With sustained effort, Italy can secure a stable fiscal path while fostering inclusive and sustainable economic growth.

Investment Opportunities: Green Transition, Digitalization, and Infrastructure

Despite fiscal challenges, Italy presents a compelling landscape for investment in key sectors, including green energy, digital transformation, and infrastructure development. With support from the EU's Next Generation Funds and strategic initiatives under the National Recovery and Resilience Plan (NRRP), the country is positioned to attract substantial private sector involvement in areas crucial for sustainable and inclusive growth.

Green Energy and Sustainability

Italy is at the forefront of Europe's green transition, leveraging its natural resources and policy frameworks to accelerate the shift to renewable energy and sustainable practices. There are significant investment opportunities in this sector, driven by both domestic initiatives and EU funding.

Renewable Energy Expansion: Investments in solar and wind energy are increasing rapidly, bolstered by government incentives and the strategic use of Next Generation EU funds. Italy is focusing on expanding its renewable energy capacity to reduce dependence on fossil fuels and achieve its ambitious climate targets. This includes scaling up large-scale solar farms, offshore and onshore wind power projects, and advancements in grid modernization to support renewable integration.

Energy Efficiency Projects: The Italian government has introduced programs to incentivize energy efficiency improvements in residential and commercial buildings.

These include the "Superbonus" tax credit, which has facilitated upgrades in energy systems, and other subsidies aimed at enhancing energy performance. These initiatives create opportunities for companies specializing in green construction, smart energy technologies, and energy-efficient equipment.

Green Hydrogen and Emerging Technologies: Italy is investing in innovative technologies such as green hydrogen production, with support for pilot projects and infrastructure development. The country's industrial base offers further potential for sustainable manufacturing and green supply chains, creating opportunities for investors aligned with environmental, social, and governance (ESG) principles.

Digital Transformation

Italy's digital economy is undergoing significant transformation, with investments in digital infrastructure, fintech, and innovation-driven growth areas. There are several opportunities in this dynamic sector, fueled by the NRRP and growing private-sector involvement.

Digital Infrastructure: Investments in high-speed broadband, 5G networks, and digital public services are central to Italy's digitalization agenda. The government's "Italy Digital 2026" plan aims to close the digital divide by expanding internet access to underserved regions, thereby creating a fertile environment for telecommunication companies and tech investors.

Fintech and Blockchain: Italy's fintech sector is growing rapidly, with opportunities in mobile payments, digital wallets, and blockchain applications. Recent regulatory advancements have improved the ecosystem for fintech startups, while traditional financial institutions are increasingly adopting technology-driven solutions to remain competitive.

Cybersecurity and AI Development: As digitalization expands, so does the demand for robust cybersecurity measures and artificial intelligence (AI) applications. Italy's focus on secure digital services and data protection presents a burgeoning market for companies offering innovative cybersecurity solutions and AI-driven technologies in sectors such as healthcare, logistics, and education.

E-Governance: The digitization of public services, including digital identity platforms and e-governance tools, is a priority for Italy. This shift not only improves efficiency but also creates opportunities for IT service providers, software developers, and cloud computing firms.

Infrastructure and Real Estate

Italy's infrastructure sector remains a cornerstone of investment opportunities, particularly in transportation, housing, and urban development. Public-private partnerships and EU financing under the NRRP are driving projects that aim to modernize Italy's infrastructure and address longstanding challenges.

Transportation Infrastructure: Italy's strategic location as a gateway between Europe and the Mediterranean makes investments in transportation infrastructure highly attractive. Projects include the modernization of railways, expansion of ports, and enhancements to urban transit systems. These initiatives offer long-term growth opportunities for construction firms, logistics companies, and investors focused on sustainable mobility.

Housing Development: Rising real estate costs in major cities like Rome and Milan underscore the need for affordable housing solutions. The growing demand for residential projects that cater to low- and middle-income families is noticeable. Opportunities also exist in sustainable housing developments, which integrate energy efficiency and smart home technologies.

Urban Regeneration: Revitalization of urban centers is a key focus of Italy's infrastructure strategy. Investments in smart cities, eco-friendly public spaces, and resilient urban planning are attracting both public and private capital. Italy's historical and cultural heritage further offers niche opportunities in adaptive reuse of old structures, blending modernization with preservation.

Energy and Transport Networks: Investments in energy and transport networks, particularly through the expansion of smart grids and electric vehicle charging stations, align with Italy's sustainability goals. These sectors are ripe for innovation and attract private equity and institutional investors seeking steady, long-term returns.

Policy Support and Incentives for Investment

Italy's investment climate is significantly bolstered by government incentives and EU funding programs. These include:

- Tax credits and subsidies for renewable energy, digitalization, and construction.

- EU grants under the NRRP that mitigate initial capital risks for large-scale infrastructure projects.

- Streamlined permitting processes and public-private collaboration frameworks to accelerate project implementation.

Italy's ongoing transformation, driven by the green transition, digitalization, and infrastructure renewal, creates a diversified landscape of opportunities for both domestic and international investors. While challenges remain, such as ensuring fiscal stability and overcoming bureaucratic inefficiencies, the strategic deployment of EU funds and government reforms are fostering an increasingly favorable environment for sustainable investment.

Conclusion: A Resilient Economy with Promising Investment Potential

Italy's economic and investment landscape in 2024 reflects a country navigating complex challenges while leveraging significant opportunities for growth and transformation. Despite moderate GDP growth and structural hurdles such as weak productivity, demographic pressures, and fiscal constraints, Italy demonstrates resilience in key areas. Its recovery from recent shocks and strategic focus on green and digital transitions, infrastructure development, and private sector innovation underscore the country's potential to attract both domestic and international investment.

The green energy sector showcases Italy's leadership in Europe's sustainability initiatives, supported by the EU's Next Generation Funds and innovative programs such as the Superbonus. Renewable energy projects, energy efficiency improvements, and cutting-edge green technologies like hydrogen offer sustainable, high-impact investment prospects. In parallel, Italy's digital transformation, backed by ambitious national strategies and NRRP funding, creates dynamic opportunities in areas ranging from fintech and cybersecurity to e-governance and AI.

Infrastructure and urban development continue to serve as pillars of Italy's investment appeal. With a robust pipeline of projects in transportation, housing, and urban regeneration, coupled with public-private partnerships, Italy is making strides in modernizing its physical and digital connectivity. Investments in sustainable housing, smart grids, and electric vehicle infrastructure align with long-term environmental and economic objectives.

However, realizing this potential requires addressing structural weaknesses. Italy must continue its fiscal consolidation efforts, improve efficiency in public spending, and implement critical reforms in taxation, pensions, and public administration. These measures will be vital in ensuring fiscal sustainability and creating a stable environment for growth.

Italy's economic outlook hinges on its ability to sustain reforms, fully leverage EU funding, and mitigate external risks such as energy market volatility and geopolitical tensions. While challenges persist, Italy's proactive policies and strategic initiatives position it as an attractive destination for investment and a key player in Europe's economic transformation. By balancing fiscal prudence with forward-looking investments, Italy can secure a path toward inclusive and sustainable growth, offering promising opportunities for stakeholders across sectors.

Chapter (4)

Spain: A Recovering Economy with Growing Investment Potential Amid Challenges

Spain, located in Southwestern Europe, has an area of approximately 505,992 square kilometres and a population of around 47.7 million people in 2024. The country's economy is projected to grow by 2.4% in FY24, driven primarily by strong domestic demand. The nominal GDP for 2024 is estimated at €1.55 trillion.

Spain's economy in 2024 reflects a remarkable balance between resilience and challenges, with a clear focus on fiscal consolidation, a green energy transition, and digital transformation. Despite facing political fragmentation and structural vulnerabilities, Spain offers a robust investment landscape that promises long-term growth for those who align with its strategic objectives. The IMF's recent consultation report sheds light on Spain's progress, as well as the investment opportunities and risks that come with its trajectory over the next few years.

Economic Outlook: Resilience Amid Uncertainty

Spain's economic outlook for 2024 remains favorable, with real GDP growth projected to reach 2.4%. After a solid 2.5% expansion in 2023, driven by resilient domestic consumption, services exports, and public spending, Spain's economy is expected to moderate slightly in 2024 but remain strong compared to the Eurozone average. This growth reflects a robust external sector, characterized by record levels of services exports, particularly in tourism and other non-tourism services, supported by sustained competitiveness gains. However, key risks persist, including political fragmentation, global geopolitical tensions, and the potential under-execution of European recovery funds. These risks could undermine confidence and weigh on growth, particularly if domestic political uncertainties further disrupt fiscal and structural reform implementation.

Private Consumption and Investment

Household consumption, bolstered by strong wage growth and a reduction in unemployment, is anticipated to sustain economic activity, with real wage gains and the gradual normalization of the savings rate supporting consumer spending. However, private investment continues to lag behind pre-pandemic levels. Despite improvements in corporate balance sheets and the increased availability of European funds, private investment has yet to fully recover, reflecting broader structural issues in Spain's investment environment. There is a potential for stronger private sector investment, particularly in productivity-enhancing areas, as financial conditions ease and confidence improves. The disbursement of Next Generation EU (NGEU) funds presents a critical opportunity to address these shortcomings and stimulate growth.

Labor Market

Spain's labor market has shown remarkable resilience, with employment growth continuing at a steady pace. The unemployment rate declined to below 12% in 2023, and the labor market reforms enacted in 2021 have significantly reduced temporary contracts, enhancing job stability. However, structural unemployment remains the highest in the Eurozone, reflecting ongoing challenges such as skills mismatches and insufficient participation among older workers. Efforts to address these issues, including enhanced active labor market policies and targeted training initiatives, are essential to improve labor market outcomes and support long-term economic convergence with higher-income Eurozone peers. Meanwhile, the tight labor market has helped moderate wage pressures, aligning nominal wage growth with productivity improvements and underpinning Spain's external competitiveness.

Inflation and Price Stability: Heading Toward ECB Targets

Inflation in Spain has significantly moderated from the peaks of 2022, marking a return to relative price stability. Headline inflation dropped to 3.4% in 2023, a sharp decline from the 8.3% observed in 2022, primarily driven by easing energy prices and a normalization of supply chain disruptions. Core inflation, which excludes volatile components such as energy and food prices, has also been on a steady downward trajectory. This reflects the gradual pass-through of lower energy costs to non-energy goods and processed food, supported by relatively moderate wage pressures despite a tight labor market.

It is projected that both headline and core inflation to converge toward the European Central Bank's (ECB) 2% target by mid-2025. This optimistic forecast hinges on several factors, including the absence of major new energy price shocks, continued monetary tightening by the ECB, and the absence of widespread wage indexation mechanisms that could trigger a wage-price spiral. The recent national wage agreement, limiting annual increases to 3% in 2024 and 2025, is expected to help anchor inflation expectations and prevent a resurgence of inflationary pressures.

This decline in inflation is critical for creating a stable environment conducive to investment and economic planning. Lower inflation enhances purchasing power and reduces uncertainty for businesses, bolstering consumer confidence and encouraging longer-term investments. However, several upside risks to inflation that could disrupt this trajectory could occur. These risks include potential increases in global energy prices due to geopolitical tensions, as well as domestic factors such as stronger-than-expected wage growth driven by labor market tightness and ongoing structural mismatches in skills and job locations.

Additionally, temporary measures, such as reduced VAT rates on essential goods, could lead to localized price increases as they are withdrawn. This underscores the importance of monitoring fiscal policy shifts and their impact on inflation. While inflationary pressures are expected to recede in the medium term, the combination of external volatility in energy markets and internal labor cost dynamics warrants close attention from policymakers and investors alike. These factors could introduce short-term fluctuations in price levels, potentially affecting Spain's broader economic climate.

By maintaining a disciplined fiscal stance and advancing structural reforms, Spain can solidify its progress toward price stability, enhancing its appeal as a destination for investment and aligning with the broader monetary goals of the Eurozone.

Fiscal Policy: Balancing Consolidation with Growth Support

Spain's fiscal policy remains focused on reducing the budget deficit and public debt, which stood at a substantial 107.7% of GDP in 2023. Despite these high levels, the country has demonstrated notable progress in fiscal consolidation. The fiscal deficit decreased significantly from 4.7% of GDP in 2022 to 3.6% in 2023, underpinned by buoyant tax revenues and strong economic growth. The government aims to reduce the deficit further to 3% in 2024, aligning with the thresholds set by the EU fiscal framework. However, achieving this goal and sustaining long-term fiscal stability will require a comprehensive and strategic approach.

Challenges in Fiscal Consolidation

It is of critical importance of Spain adopting a credible medium-term fiscal consolidation plan to ensure debt sustainability. Without such a plan, the country risks continued exposure to fiscal vulnerabilities. Public expenditure pressures are mounting, particularly in pensions and healthcare, due to the aging population. Recent pension reforms, which indexed benefits to inflation, have increased long-term fiscal commitments. While these changes aim to protect retirees' purchasing power, they could place significant strain on public finances unless offset by additional revenue measures or adjustments in benefit levels.

On the revenue side, Spain has benefited from strong tax collection driven by employment growth and higher nominal wages. Increased personal income taxes and social security contributions have played a key role in fiscal improvement. However, relying solely on revenue measures is insufficient. Structural reforms, particularly in the pension system, are crucial to contain expenditure growth. Options include extending the computation period for pension benefits to align with full career earnings and encouraging delayed retirement through enhanced incentives. Absent these reforms, long-term fiscal strain could escalate, jeopardizing Spain's economic stability.

Political Risks

Spain's fiscal trajectory is heavily influenced by its complex political landscape. the fragmented political environment, characterized by difficulties in forming stable coalitions and passing legislation, presents a significant obstacle to effective fiscal policymaking. The complexities associated with passing a budget law for 2024 exemplifies these challenges, as the government must operate under a "rollover" of the previous year's budget. This approach limits flexibility and may delay critical reforms and investment initiatives.

Furthermore, the absence of a detailed medium-term fiscal plan as a key weakness. Such a plan would anchor fiscal consolidation efforts and signal the government's commitment to addressing long-term challenges, such as debt reduction and expenditure pressures. Political fragmentation could also undermine the implementation of necessary structural reforms, including those targeting pensions and healthcare, as well as measures to optimize the use of EU recovery funds. These factors collectively increase the risk of fiscal slippage, particularly if economic growth weakens or external shocks arise.

While Spain has made meaningful strides in fiscal consolidation, sustained progress will require balancing near-term fiscal discipline with long-term structural reforms. The need for a clear and actionable fiscal strategy that integrates expenditure containment, particularly in pensions, with growth-friendly revenue measures such as broadening the tax base and enhancing environmental taxation is paramount. Addressing the challenges posed by political fragmentation will be essential to maintaining fiscal momentum and ensuring that Spain's fiscal policy supports both economic stability and growth over the medium term.

Investment Opportunities: Green Transition, Digitalization, and Infrastructure

Despite fiscal and political challenges, Spain presents robust investment opportunities, particularly in green energy, digital transformation, and infrastructure. The strategic deployment of Next Generation EU (NGEU) funds amplifies these prospects, enabling significant advancements in key sectors.

Green Transition and Renewable Energy

Spain's commitment to the green transition has positioned the country as a European leader in renewable energy, particularly in solar and wind power. In 2023, Spain further expanded its renewable energy capacity, driven by public policies aligned with EU climate goals. Spain's effective use of NGEU funds to accelerate the deployment of clean technologies, enhance energy efficiency, and develop sustainable infrastructure. Initiatives like retrofitting buildings for energy efficiency and scaling up electric vehicle infrastructure underscore Spain's ambition to achieve a low-carbon economy.

Additionally, Spain's strategic location and natural resources make it a potential hub for green hydrogen production, which has garnered increasing interest from global investors. Spain's focus on decarbonization is complemented by strong public-private partnerships aimed at fostering innovation and scaling up renewable energy projects. This creates fertile ground for investment in renewable energy production, storage, and grid modernization.

Green Bonds and Sustainable Finance

Spain's green bond market continues to expand, offering investors opportunities to participate in sustainable projects. The government and private sector have both utilized green bonds to finance renewable energy and infrastructure initiatives. Spain has benefitted from the EU's green taxonomy, which provides clear standards for sustainable investments, enhancing investor confidence.

The rising demand for sustainable finance products has also spurred innovation in the broader financial market, with Spain's financial institutions actively developing ESG (Environmental, Social, and Governance) products tailored to investor needs. Spain's commitment to EU-wide sustainability goals further ensures that the green finance market will continue to grow, providing stable, long-term returns for investors.

Digital Economy and Innovation

Spain is accelerating its digital transformation, underpinned by significant investments in technology, fintech, and digital infrastructure. The deployment of NGEU funds has catalyzed digitalization across public and private sectors. Investments in broadband expansion, 5G networks, and the digitization of public services are creating a solid foundation for a modern, innovation-driven economy.

The financial sector is at the forefront of digitalization, with initiatives aimed at enhancing cybersecurity, promoting digital banking, and increasing access to financial services. These developments are supported by Spain's emphasis on public-private collaboration to strengthen the digital ecosystem. Moreover, the government's strategic push for digital transformation creates a favorable environment for investments in artificial intelligence, cloud computing, and other cutting-edge technologies.

Fintech Growth

Spain's burgeoning fintech sector offers a wealth of opportunities for investors. Supported by NGEU funds and a focus on financial inclusion, the country has witnessed strong growth in digital payment systems and blockchain applications. Spain's investments in mobile payments and advanced digital payment infrastructure align with global trends, positioning the country as a leader in digital finance innovation. The fintech ecosystem's growth also presents opportunities in areas such as digital wallets, cryptocurrency, and cybersecurity solutions, driven by increasing consumer adoption of digital financial services.

Infrastructure Investment

Spain's infrastructure sector remains a cornerstone of its investment landscape, particularly in transportation, urban development, and housing. The critical need to expand Spain's housing supply to address rising affordability concerns, especially in urban centers is essential. Investments in affordable housing and urban renewal projects present attractive avenues for long-term private capital, addressing pressing social needs while offering stable returns.

Public transportation projects, such as high-speed rail and urban transit systems, are also priorities under Spain's recovery plan. Sustainable urban development, including the integration of green technologies in public infrastructure projects is vital. Spain's infrastructure initiatives, supported by EU funds and private partnerships, provide opportunities for investment in transformative projects that enhance connectivity, sustainability, and economic growth.

By leveraging EU funds and aligning with global trends in sustainability and digitalization, Spain continues to offer a diverse array of high-potential investment opportunities. Investors seeking long-term returns in sectors poised for growth will find Spain's commitment to transformation a compelling prospect.

Risks to Investment: Political and Structural Challenges

While Spain offers compelling investment opportunities, potential investors must be mindful of several risks that could impact economic stability and investment returns.

Political Fragmentation

Spain's fragmented political landscape continues to pose challenges to the stability and implementation of economic policies. The inability to pass a 2024 budget exemplifies the difficulties of securing political consensus in a divided parliament. This political uncertainty can delay critical reforms, including those related to pensions, taxation, and housing, increasing regulatory uncertainty for businesses and investors. Fragmentation also heightens the risk of under-execution of European recovery funds, which are crucial for advancing infrastructure and green energy projects. Ongoing

political deadlock may undermine investor confidence and
deter long-term capital inflows.

Fiscal and Debt Pressures

Spain's high public debt, which stood at 107.7% of GDP in
2023, and its rising social spending, particularly in pensions
and healthcare, represent significant long-term fiscal
challenges. Without structural reforms to control spending,
the country risks further fiscal strain as the population ages
and healthcare demands grow. Recent reforms indexing
pensions to inflation, while beneficial for retirees, exacerbate
long-term fiscal imbalances are critical.

Additionally, while tax revenues have increased due to strong
employment growth and higher wages, relying on revenue
measures alone is not sustainable. Rising borrowing costs,
driven by higher global interest rates and Spain's elevated
debt levels, could increase the cost of financing, limiting
fiscal flexibility and eroding investor confidence. These fiscal
pressures could also crowd out public investment in areas
critical to economic growth, such as infrastructure and
innovation.

Global Risks

Spain's open economy is highly exposed to global economic
conditions, making it vulnerable to external shocks.
Fluctuations in commodity prices, particularly energy,
present ongoing risks to inflation and production costs.
Geopolitical tensions, such as conflicts affecting global
energy markets, could further exacerbate these pressures,
raising Spain's energy import costs and impacting business
operations.

As a major exporter of goods and services, Spain's economy is sensitive to disruptions in global trade and supply chains. Slowdowns in key trading partners, such as the Eurozone or the United States, could negatively affect Spain's export sectors, particularly in automotive, machinery, and tourism. Furthermore, the country's reliance on foreign capital inflows makes it susceptible to shifts in global investor sentiment, particularly if geopolitical or financial instability increases.

Investors considering opportunities in Spain should weigh these risks alongside the country's strengths. While Spain's political and fiscal challenges require vigilance, continued progress in structural reforms, effective deployment of EU funds, and resilience in key sectors such as digitalization and green energy can help mitigate these risks. However, careful monitoring of global economic trends and domestic policy developments will be essential for investors to navigate Spain's dynamic investment environment effectively.

Conclusion: A Mixed but Promising Investment Landscape

Spain stands at a pivotal crossroads, presenting a complex yet promising economic landscape for investors and policymakers alike. Its resilience in the face of global uncertainty, underpinned by robust economic growth, a recovering labor market, and a focused transition toward green and digital economies, highlights the country's potential as a key player in the Eurozone. Investment opportunities abound in renewable energy, digital transformation, and infrastructure, all supported by substantial EU funding and strategic public-private initiatives.

However, navigating Spain's investment terrain requires an astute awareness of its challenges. Political fragmentation, fiscal pressures, and exposure to global risks underscore the importance of informed decision-making and adaptive strategies. The country's ability to sustain its momentum will depend on implementing structural reforms, mitigating fiscal vulnerabilities, and fostering an environment of political stability.

For those willing to embrace both the opportunities and risks, Spain offers a unique chance to be part of a transformative journey. Its commitment to innovation, sustainability, and economic modernization positions it not only as a recovering economy but as a resilient and dynamic hub for long-term growth. By aligning with Spain's strategic objectives, investors can play a pivotal role in shaping a brighter economic future while reaping the rewards of a nation on the rise.

Chapter (5)

Netherlands: A Strategic Economic and Investment Landscape Amid Transition

The Netherlands, located in Western Europe, covers an area of approximately 41,543 square kilometres and has a population of around 17.7 million people in 2024. The country's economy is projected to grow by 0.6% in FY24, following a period of slower growth. The nominal GDP for 2024 is estimated at approximately €950 billion, with growth driven by private consumption and stronger external demand.

The Dutch economy, resilient yet facing critical crossroads, has shown flexibility in recent years, especially during the pandemic. Today, the Netherlands balances emerging economic opportunities with distinct challenges across inflation, climate policy, and fiscal sustainability. With insights from the IMF's 2024 Article IV consultation, the following overview explores the Netherlands' economic trajectory and investment potential amid its transformative policies in fiscal management, green technology, and digital advancement.

Steady Economic Recovery and Inflation Challenges

In 2023, the Netherlands experienced a significant cooling in economic growth, registering a minimal 0.1% increase. This deceleration was primarily attributed to the aftermath of higher energy costs, tighter financial conditions, and subdued demand from key trading partners, notably Germany. The Dutch economy faced contractions in private consumption during the first half of the year, driven by eroding consumer purchasing power, sluggish industrial production, and reduced exports. However, positive signs emerged in the final quarter of 2023, with modest improvements in real wages and a slight rebound in house prices. Despite these challenges, the Netherlands displayed resilience, aided by its strong economic fundamentals. Growth is projected to recover gradually to 0.6% in 2024 and 1.3% by 2025, supported by improved household purchasing power and stronger external demand, even as high interest rates continue to weigh on investments.

Inflation Dynamics:

Core inflation in the Netherlands remains elevated, driven by persistent wage pressures and robust corporate profit margins, which together sustain upward price trends despite the cooling economy. By December 2023, adjusted HICP inflation had declined significantly to 2.2%, reflecting a reduction in energy price shocks. The headline inflation rate is expected to ease further to 2.7% in 2024 and align with the European Central Bank's target of 2% by mid-2025. Nonetheless, risks of inflation persistence exist, especially if wage growth accelerates in response to a tight labor market.

To counteract potential second-round effects, a cautious fiscal stance is recommended. Measures such as unwinding untargeted energy subsidies, rationalizing fossil fuel subsidies, and prioritizing deficit reduction could help align inflation with medium-term targets while safeguarding fiscal sustainability.

Labor Market Robustness:

The Dutch labor market continues to demonstrate exceptional robustness despite broader economic challenges. Unemployment remained low at 3.6% in late 2023, with the participation rate reaching 75.9%, the highest in the Euro Area. However, the labor market faces structural challenges, including widespread shortages across multiple sectors and high job vacancy rates. Real wages, although improving due to declining inflation, remain below pre-pandemic levels, while the risk of a wage-price spiral is contained. Tackling labor shortages will require comprehensive reforms, including:

- Encouraging part-time workers to increase working hours by improving child and elder care systems.

- Promoting training and labor mobility toward sectors crucial for the green and digital transitions.

- Streamlining tax-benefit systems to incentivize workforce participation.

- Adopting advanced technologies, including AI, to boost productivity while optimizing migration policies to address skill gaps.

Strategic investments in digitalization and green technologies
are also crucial to enhance labor market resilience and sustain
economic growth. The Netherlands' commitment to
addressing these challenges through structural reforms
underscores its potential for recovery and sustained long-
term growth.

Fiscal Policies: Balancing Expansion and Sustainability

Fiscal policy in the Netherlands has been cautiously
expansionary, driven by targeted social support and public
investment. However, future spending pressures on
healthcare, pensions, and defense, alongside commitments to
climate and energy transitions, necessitate strategic
adjustments to ensure long-term fiscal sustainability. The
following priorities are recommended:

Debt Stability and Structural Adjustments

While the Netherlands' public debt ratio is low compared to
its European peers, long-term spending pressures present
challenges that require proactive measures. Healthcare
expenditures are projected to rise from 9.5% to 10.5% of
GDP by 2028, while pension spending is expected to grow
from 4.6% to 5.2% of GDP. Defense spending is also set to
increase significantly, reaching 2% of GDP by 2028, aligning
with NATO commitments. To stabilize public debt at its
projected 2028 level, a phased deficit reduction averaging
0.3% of GDP annually. This adjustment can be achieved
through:

Tax Reforms: Streamlining inefficient tax expenditures, including reductions in VAT exemptions and adjustments to tax treatment for owner-occupied housing, can enhance revenue while preserving equity.

Spending Efficiency: Addressing structural inefficiencies in healthcare, such as optimizing the basic policy package and exploring co-payment mechanisms, and linking the retirement age more closely to life expectancy can mitigate cost escalations.

Investment Prioritization: Maintaining or increasing investment in key areas like housing, education, and the green transition ensures that fiscal consolidation does not compromise long-term growth prospects.

Streamlining Energy Subsidies

The Netherlands has made strides in aligning its fiscal policies with its environmental commitments by cutting implicit fossil fuel subsidies, which currently represent 4–5% of GDP. There is a clear need to phase out untargeted energy subsidies that disproportionately benefit higher-income households. By reallocating these resources, fiscal space can be created to fund targeted social programs, such as energy relief for vulnerable households, and to bolster investments in renewable energy infrastructure. Recent budgetary measures have already eliminated €6 billion in such subsidies, demonstrating the feasibility and impact of this strategy.

It is imperative to integrate carbon pricing and feebate systems to complement subsidy reductions. These measures, which incentivize lower emissions through pricing and rebates, are expected to enhance the efficiency of the Netherlands' transition to a greener economy while maintaining robust fiscal revenues.

Fiscal Agility Amid Uncertainty

Given high global and domestic uncertainties, fiscal policy should remain flexible to respond to emerging risks. For instance, a sharp correction in the housing market may necessitate discretionary fiscal support, while persistent inflationary pressures could require more aggressive fiscal adjustments to prevent overheating. Automatic stabilizers, such as unemployment benefits and progressive taxation, will play a critical role in moderating the impact of economic shocks.

Strategically balancing fiscal expansion with sustainability will enable the Netherlands to address long-term challenges while ensuring resilience to near-term risks, setting a foundation for sustained growth and environmental stewardship.

Green and Digital Transitions: Investment in Sustainability and Innovation

The Netherlands has set ambitious targets for its green and digital transitions, aiming to lead in sustainable development and technological innovation. These dual transformations prioritize strategic investment in renewable energy, digital infrastructure, and sustainable urban development, laying the groundwork for long-term economic resilience and competitiveness.

Climate and Energy Initiatives

As part of its commitment to achieving a 60% reduction in greenhouse gas emissions by 2030, the Netherlands has implemented a comprehensive strategy that balances environmental and economic priorities. This includes:

Subsidy Reforms: Efforts to phase out implicit fossil fuel subsidies, which currently account for 4–5% of GDP, are ongoing. Recent cuts of €6 billion in such subsidies in the 2024 budget have freed up fiscal resources for green investments and targeted social support, such as energy relief programs for vulnerable households. These reforms not only align with climate goals but also enhance fiscal sustainability.

Carbon Pricing and Emissions Standards: The Netherlands is leveraging the EU's emissions trading system while introducing domestic measures to incentivize clean energy adoption. This includes carbon pricing in sectors like mobility and agriculture and stricter standards for energy efficiency and emissions reduction in the industrial sector.

Renewable Energy Expansion: The Netherlands leads globally in per capita rooftop solar panel installations and hosts 24% of Europe's electric vehicle charging stations. The government is also accelerating the transition to green gas, targeting a 20% increase in production by 2030. These initiatives provide significant investment opportunities in renewable energy markets, particularly solar and wind power, and the broader green technology ecosystem.

Sustainable Urban Planning: Urban centers are embracing smart city technologies, green infrastructure, and sustainable housing solutions, offering investment potential in energy-efficient buildings and climate-resilient infrastructure.

Digitalization Strategy

The Netherlands views its digital transition as a critical lever for addressing labor shortages and boosting economic productivity. The government has prioritized investments in cutting-edge digital infrastructure, with a focus on:

5G Networks and Automation: Rapid deployment of 5G technology is enhancing connectivity and enabling advancements in automation and artificial intelligence (AI). These technologies are pivotal for industries ranging from manufacturing to healthcare, fostering a tech-driven economy with high productivity and innovation.

Skill Development for the Digital Era: To address skill mismatches in the labor market, the Netherlands is investing in training programs that equip workers with expertise in digital technologies, including AI, data analytics, and cybersecurity. These efforts aim to ensure that the workforce can meet the demands of a rapidly digitalizing economy.

Incentives for Digital Transformation: The government is encouraging businesses to adopt digital solutions through tax incentives and grants, making it an attractive destination for local and international tech investors. Support for startups and innovation hubs further strengthens its position as a digital leader.

Financial Sector Stability and Housing Market Adjustments

The Dutch financial sector demonstrates significant resilience, underpinned by robust banking systems and proactive regulatory measures. However, heightened risks, particularly in the real estate market, underscore the importance of vigilant oversight.

Banking Resilience

The Dutch banking sector remains well-capitalized and liquid, with profitability metrics that outpace many European peers. Key indicators include:

Strong Capital Buffers: Dutch banks maintain high Common Equity Tier 1 (CET1) ratios, ensuring the capacity to absorb shocks. As of 2023, banks also benefited from enhanced countercyclical capital buffers set at 2%, effective May 2024.

Resilience to Economic Stress: While non-performing loan (NPL) ratios remain low, potential risks from high household and corporate debt persist, particularly in scenarios of prolonged interest rate increases. Real estate loans, comprising a significant share of banks' portfolios, represent a key area of sensitivity to economic downturns or corrections in property prices.

Macroprudential Policies: To mitigate systemic risks, the Netherlands has implemented borrower-based measures, such as risk weight floors for mortgages and limits on interest-only loans. Further adjustments are encouraged, including reducing maximum loan-to-value (LTV) ratios from the current 100% to 90% over time, to enhance resilience against real estate market corrections.

Housing Market and Affordability

The housing market in the Netherlands continues to face challenges characterized by high demand, constrained supply, and affordability issues:

Housing Shortage and Prices: The Netherlands grapples with a structural housing shortage, which has driven up property prices significantly over the past decade. Despite recent corrections, prices remain elevated, exacerbating affordability concerns, particularly for younger and lower-income households.

Affordability Policies: Recommendations to adopt a balanced approach to address such challenges include:

- **Gradual LTV Reductions:** Lowering LTV ratios would reduce household vulnerabilities and promote more sustainable borrowing practices.
- **Tax Reforms:** Rationalizing tax benefits, such as the mortgage interest deduction, could address distortions in the housing market and reduce demand pressures.
- **Incentivizing Housing Supply:** Streamlining permitting processes and increasing investment in housing infrastructure are critical to addressing the housing shortage. Policies encouraging public-private partnerships can expedite construction and improve market balance.

Broader Financial Stability Considerations

Beyond the banking and housing sectors, other financial vulnerabilities require attention:

Non-Bank Financial Institutions (NBFIs): These entities, including pension funds and insurers, face risks from market volatility, liquidity pressures, and climate-related exposures. Ongoing efforts to enhance supervisory frameworks and improve risk management across the financial sector should be supported.

Climate Risks: Rising sea levels and extreme weather events pose challenges for the financial system. Banks and insurers must integrate climate risk assessments into their operations, while policymakers should continue to refine climate-related macroprudential tools.

Policy Recommendations for Stability

To ensure long-term stability, several policy priorities are recommended:

- Enhance access to granular, loan-level data to improve risk assessments in the real estate sector.

- Continue adjusting macroprudential measures to address risks stemming from elevated household debt and high real estate exposures.

- Invest in climate resilience measures to mitigate financial risks from physical and transition climate impacts.

- Strengthen frameworks for crisis preparedness and resolution to address potential shocks.

By addressing these areas, the Netherlands can maintain its strong financial stability while creating a more equitable and resilient housing market. These efforts will also contribute to broader economic stability and growth.

Strategic Sectors for Investment: Opportunities in Green Tech, Digital, and Healthcare

The Dutch economy's investment landscape is characterized by its diversification and forward-thinking approach, particularly in sectors pivotal to the global economy. With government-backed incentives and robust frameworks, the Netherlands is an attractive destination for investors in renewable energy, digital infrastructure, and healthcare innovation.

Renewable Energy and Green Technologies

The Netherlands is at the forefront of renewable energy development, driven by ambitious climate goals to reduce greenhouse gas emissions by 60% by 2030. Key areas of opportunity include:

Solar and Wind Energy: With the highest per capita rooftop solar installations globally and a strong emphasis on offshore wind projects, the Netherlands offers extensive investment opportunities in clean energy production.

Energy Storage and Grid Upgrades: As renewable energy adoption increases, investments in energy storage solutions and grid modernization are critical to managing supply volatility and enhancing efficiency.

Circular Economy and Green Innovation: Government incentives support innovations in recycling, sustainable manufacturing, and green building technologies, aligning with global trends in environmental sustainability.

Digital Infrastructure and Automation

Digital transformation is central to the Netherlands' economic strategy, targeting improved efficiency, productivity, and solutions to labor shortages. Investment opportunities include:

Advanced Technologies: Artificial intelligence (AI), cybersecurity, and Internet of Things (IoT) solutions are rapidly gaining traction across industries, offering high-growth potential for tech investors.

5G Deployment: Continued expansion of 5G infrastructure provides opportunities in telecommunications and supports the adoption of emerging technologies in sectors such as logistics and healthcare.

Digitalization of SMEs: Government programs promoting digital adoption among small and medium enterprises (SMEs) offer avenues for investment in software, platforms, and training solutions tailored to this segment.

Healthcare Innovation

As the Dutch population ages, healthcare is emerging as a critical area for investment, driven by rising demand for advanced services and technologies. Prominent opportunities include:

Biotechnology and Pharmaceuticals: The Netherlands' strong research and development ecosystem supports the growth of biotechnology and innovative drug development.

Telemedicine and Digital Health: Investments in telemedicine platforms, remote patient monitoring, and data-driven health solutions are gaining momentum as healthcare systems adapt to new challenges.

Elderly Care Solutions: Innovations in elderly care, including robotics, assistive devices, and sustainable housing solutions, align with the growing demand for specialized services.

Key Takeaways for Investors

The Netherlands presents a dynamic and evolving economic landscape where sustainability and innovation are pivotal to growth. While the country's strategic focus on green and digital transitions offers significant opportunities, investors must remain cognizant of fiscal pressures and potential policy adjustments that may impact returns. The following insights can guide strategic investment decisions:

Focus on Policy-Aligned Sectors

Investments in sectors that align with government priorities and benefit from policy incentives are well-positioned for growth. Key opportunities include:

Green Technology: Robust support for renewable energy projects, including solar, wind, and green hydrogen, as well as initiatives in circular economy practices, ensures a conducive environment for sustainable investments.

Digital Infrastructure: The Netherlands' focus on enhancing digital connectivity through 5G deployment, AI development, and automation creates profitable pathways for technology-driven investments.

Healthcare Innovation: Government-backed reforms in healthcare, coupled with rising demand for biotechnology, telemedicine, and elderly care solutions, make this sector a lucrative investment avenue.

Long-Term Vision for Sustainable Growth

The Netherlands' emphasis on climate action and digitalization aligns with global Environmental, Social, and Governance (ESG) trends, which are increasingly influencing investment strategies. The country's commitment to reducing greenhouse gas emissions by 60% by 2030 and fostering a tech-driven economy offers a framework for sustained and resilient returns. Investors with a long-term perspective can capitalize on:

> Opportunities in energy storage, grid modernization, and energy-efficient buildings.

- Digitalization efforts across sectors, particularly those enhancing productivity and addressing labor shortages.

- Sustainable investments in public and private infrastructure projects that align with ESG principles.

Caution in Financial and Real Estate Investments

Heightened risks in the real estate sector, coupled with broader financial vulnerabilities, necessitate a cautious approach. Key considerations include:

Real Estate Market Sensitivity: Elevated property prices, despite recent corrections, and the potential for further adjustments underscore the need for prudent investment strategies. Monitoring government policies on mortgage loan-to-value (LTV) ratios, housing supply, and tax reforms is essential.

Macroprudential Regulation: The financial sector's exposure to real estate and high household debt requires vigilance. Investors should stay informed about regulatory adjustments, such as capital buffer requirements and borrower-based measures, which could impact market dynamics.

The Netherlands' Path Forward: An Era of Resilience and Innovation

The Netherlands stands as a beacon of resilience and innovation amidst a rapidly evolving global landscape. With its steadfast commitment to sustainability, technological advancement, and fiscal prudence, the nation exemplifies the ability to balance pressing challenges with transformative opportunities. Dutch economy poised at the intersection of growth and reinvention.

From the strategic embrace of green technologies to the relentless pursuit of digital excellence, the Netherlands has carved out a niche as a leader in addressing 21st-century challenges. Its ambitious goals—whether in renewable energy expansion, urban sustainability, or healthcare innovation—serve not only as solutions to domestic priorities but also as global investment opportunities. Yet, the path forward is not without its complexities. The careful management of inflation, housing market sensitivities, and fiscal pressures will define the Netherlands' trajectory in the years ahead.

For investors, the Dutch economic landscape offers a compelling narrative of growth, resilience, and innovation. By aligning with policy-supported sectors and maintaining a long-term vision, investors can unlock opportunities that align with global Environmental, Social, and Governance (ESG) priorities. However, prudent strategies that account for real estate risks and fiscal adjustments are essential to navigating the economic transformation underway.

As the Netherlands continues to refine its policies and adapt to emerging global dynamics, it cements its role as a strategic hub for sustainable development and economic opportunity. The future of the Dutch economy is one of promise—a promise to lead, innovate, and thrive in a world in transition.

Chapter (6)

Poland: Balancing Resilience and Transformation Amid Global Challenges

Poland, located in Central Europe, has a total area of approximately 312,696 square kilometres. As of 2024, the country's population is around 38 million people. Poland's economy is projected to recover in 2024, with real GDP growth expected to reach 2.4%. The nominal GDP for FY24 is forecasted to be approximately 3.8 trillion PLN.

Poland's economy is at a turning point, grappling with challenges stemming from global shocks, structural constraints, and domestic policy adjustments. Yet, the country's steadfast resilience and ambitious reforms highlight opportunities for sustainable growth and investment. As a key player in Central and Eastern Europe, Poland navigates inflationary pressures, demographic transitions, and geopolitical uncertainties with an eye toward long-term transformation. This chapter provides an in-depth exploration of Poland's economic performance, fiscal strategy, inflation trends, and investment landscape, focusing on how reforms and strategic decisions are reshaping the nation's trajectory.

Economic Performance: A Resilient but Moderating Trajectory

A Recovery Slowed by External Shocks

Poland's economic rebound from the COVID-19 pandemic was robust, with GDP growth of 5.1% in 2022, underpinned by resilient domestic demand and effective public policy. However, the second half of 2022 saw a marked slowdown due to surging inflation, monetary policy tightening, and energy price shocks exacerbated by Russia's invasion of Ukraine. GDP growth is projected to slow significantly to 0.3% in 2023, constrained by declining real wages, sluggish consumption, and headwinds in fixed investment.

Despite near-term challenges, the outlook remains moderately optimistic. GDP is expected to rebound to 2.4% in 2024 and stabilize at approximately 3% annually over the medium term, fueled by the disbursement of EU Next Generation EU (NGEU) funds and gradual improvements in private consumption and investment. Poland's resilience is further bolstered by its integration into European and global value chains, a strong industrial base, and targeted public spending.

Labor Market Resilience and Emerging Challenges

Poland's labor market remains one of its strongest assets, with unemployment rates below 3.5%—among the lowest in the EU. This robust performance reflects structural labor shortages, an aging population, and the successful absorption of approximately one million Ukrainian refugees. However, challenges persist, including skill mismatches in high-demand sectors such as ICT, finance, and manufacturing.

While nominal wages grew by over 12% in 2022, inflation has outpaced these gains, leading to negative real wage growth and eroding household purchasing power. The government's decision to raise the minimum wage by nearly 20% in 2023 aims to address this gap, but sustaining wage growth without exacerbating inflation will require productivity-enhancing reforms and investments in education and training.

Inflation and Monetary Policy: Navigating Persistent Pressures

Inflation Dynamics

Inflation surged to an unprecedented peak of 18.4% in February 2023, driven by external shocks to energy and food prices and compounded by second-round effects and tight domestic labor markets. Government measures, such as the "Anti-Inflation Shield," provided temporary relief but masked underlying price pressures. Headline inflation is projected to average 12.4% in 2023 before moderating to 5.1% in 2024 and approaching the central bank's target of 2.5% by 2025.

Policy Interventions

The National Bank of Poland (NBP) responded decisively, raising interest rates significantly in 2021-22. While the central bank paused rate hikes in late 2022, it remains poised to tighten further if core inflation fails to decelerate as expected. Complementary fiscal measures, including targeted energy subsidies and tightened public spending, are crucial to support monetary efforts in curbing inflation without stalling economic activity.

Fiscal Policy: Balancing Growth and Sustainability

Deficits and Debt

Poland's fiscal stance has shifted toward expansionary policies in response to inflation and geopolitical shocks. The general government deficit widened to 4.5% of GDP in 2023, reflecting slowing revenue growth, increased defense spending, and ongoing energy subsidies. Public debt remains manageable at 50.2% of GDP but is projected to rise to 55% by 2027 due to higher borrowing costs and strategic spending priorities.

Fiscal consolidation will be critical to ensuring long-term sustainability. Medium-term projections suggest that debt stabilization will require structural reforms, including enhanced revenue generation and targeted expenditure cuts.

Reforming Public Finances

Several fiscal reforms are underway to improve efficiency and equity:

Tax Reforms: The government's "Polish Deal" introduced progressive income tax measures that reduced the burden on lower-income households. Moving forward, aligning corporate tax policies with EU standards, such as the adoption of a 15% minimum corporate tax rate, will bolster revenues while maintaining investor confidence.

Energy Subsidies: The 2023 "Energy Shield" includes mechanisms to incentivize energy conservation, such as block pricing and higher tariffs for excessive consumption. These measures aim to phase out broad subsidies in favor of targeted support for vulnerable households and businesses.

Social Benefits: Poland's universal benefit programs, such as the "Family 500+" scheme, are being reevaluated. Transitioning to means-tested benefits could improve targeting and reduce fiscal pressures, freeing resources for critical investments.

Investment Landscape: Opportunities Amid Transition

Energy Transition and Sustainability

Poland's energy sector is undergoing a profound transformation. The country has significantly reduced its dependence on Russian gas, leveraging LNG imports and the Baltic pipeline. Renewables, particularly wind and solar, are central to Poland's energy strategy, with EU funding driving investments in clean energy projects and infrastructure.

Challenges remain in reducing coal reliance and meeting decarbonization targets. However, the government's commitments under the EU Green Deal provide a roadmap for sustainable growth, with substantial opportunities for private and foreign investors in energy-efficient buildings, smart grids, and electric mobility.

Digital Transformation

Poland's thriving ICT sector is a cornerstone of its investment appeal. The government's Smart Specialization Strategy targets high-value industries such as AI, blockchain, and digital finance. EU-funded investments in broadband infrastructure and research and development (R&D) are expected to drive innovation, creating opportunities for startups and established firms alike. Addressing digital skill shortages through education and workforce training will be pivotal.

Real Estate and Infrastructure

The real estate market remains dynamic, driven by urbanization and housing demand. However, affordability challenges have emerged due to rising interest rates and construction costs. Government initiatives to expand public housing and streamline urban planning aim to address these concerns, offering opportunities for sustainable real estate development and infrastructure upgrades.

Structural Reforms: Unlocking Long-Term Potential

Poland's economic sustainability hinges on comprehensive reforms. Key priorities include:

Labor Market Modernization: Extending the retirement age and integrating Ukrainian refugees more fully into the workforce can mitigate demographic pressures.

Judicial Reforms: Aligning judicial practices with EU standards will unlock NGEU funds and strengthen investor confidence.

Public Sector Efficiency: Streamlining off-budget expenditures and enhancing fiscal transparency will improve governance and fiscal discipline.

Conclusion: A Vision for Sustainable Growth

Poland's economic story is one of resilience and transformation. Strategic investments in energy security, digital infrastructure, and human capital, coupled with fiscal discipline and structural reforms, are shaping a pathway to inclusive and sustainable growth. While challenges persist, Poland's proactive policies and commitment to modernization position it as a leading destination for investment in Central and Eastern Europe. By harnessing its strengths and addressing its vulnerabilities, Poland is poised to achieve a future of resilient and equitable growth.

Chapter (7)

Belgium: Navigating Challenges and Unlocking Opportunities in a Transformative Economy

Belgium, located in Western Europe, covers an area of approximately 30,528 square kilometres. As of 2024, its population is estimated at 11.7 million people. The country's economy has shown resilience, with Belgium projected to achieve a nominal GDP of €609.1 billion in 2024. However, Belgium faces several economic challenges, including an aging population, high public debt, and structural fiscal deficits.

Belgium's economy presents a unique mix of resilience, challenges, and potential. The 2023 IMF Article IV Consultation report highlights the country's response to external shocks and the pressing need for fiscal, structural, and green reforms. This chapter delves deeper into Belgium's economic trajectory, fiscal policy landscape, and sectoral opportunities, providing a comprehensive guide for investors.

Resilience Amid Challenges

Belgium has weathered a series of crises, including the COVID-19 pandemic and the energy shock, thanks to timely policy interventions. However, the economic environment has grown more challenging, with slowing growth, persistent inflation, and structural impediments. Key Economic Indicators:

Growth Moderation: Real GDP growth slowed to 1.4% in 2023, with projections of 1.0% in 2024. Medium-term growth is constrained by low productivity and labor market challenges.

Inflation Pressures: While headline inflation declined to 2.5% in 2023 from a peak of 13.1% in October 2022, core inflation remains high at 6.7%, driven by wage indexation and robust household demand.

Labor Market Dynamics: Unemployment remains low at 5.6%, but vacancy rates are among the highest in the EU, signaling structural rigidities, including skill mismatches and limited interregional mobility.

Fiscal Landscape: Challenges and Reform Imperatives

Belgium's fiscal health has faced significant setbacks, exacerbated by the pandemic and energy crises. These shocks have led to a sharp increase in public debt and persistent structural deficits. In particular, Belgium's public debt surpassed 105% of GDP in 2023 and is expected to climb to 113% by 2028, well above the EU's sustainability benchmarks. The government's ability to respond to future shocks has been compromised by the erosion of fiscal buffers, necessitating urgent reforms to restore fiscal stability and maintain Belgium's social model.

Deficit and Debt Challenges:

Fiscal Deficit: The general government deficit is projected to rise to 4.5% of GDP in 2023, driven by escalating wage costs, social benefit indexation, and spending related to Belgium's aging population. Structural deficits, including those exacerbated by rising inflation and indexation mechanisms, are projected to persist. The fiscal deficit is expected to remain elevated at around 5.5% of GDP over the medium term, putting further strain on public finances.

Public Debt: Belgium's public debt is on an unsustainable path. Although there was a temporary reduction in debt during the post-pandemic recovery period, public debt has increased again due to wider fiscal deficits, lower economic growth, and higher interest rates. It is estimated that Belgium's debt will reach 113% of GDP by 2028, a worrying trend that underscores the need for more aggressive fiscal consolidation.

Fiscal Reform Priorities:

To address these mounting challenges, Belgium must undertake comprehensive fiscal reforms, focusing on both reducing deficits and improving the efficiency of public spending.

Rationalizing Spending: Belgium's social benefits expenditure is substantially higher than the EU average for advanced economies. However, the effectiveness of these benefits is diminishing. For instance, social benefit spending is 5.2 percentage points higher than the EU advanced economy average, but the returns in terms of social outcomes are not proportionate. Temporarily pausing wage indexation and implementing efficiency gains in healthcare and pensions to curb spending while ensuring that these areas remain sustainable over the long term.

Pension Reform: Belgium has made progress with pension reforms, but more is needed. Recent measures are expected to save about 0.5% of GDP by 2070. These measures primarily focus on reducing the indexation of civil servant pensions and limiting pension increases. However, Belgium's pension system still faces substantial long-term sustainability challenges due to the aging population. The effective retirement age remains below the OECD average (63.8 years), and further reforms will be necessary to raise the effective retirement age and ensure the system's sustainability.

Healthcare Efficiency: Belgium's healthcare system, while providing excellent access to care and high health outcomes, does so at a relatively high cost. If Belgium could align its healthcare efficiency with OECD standards, it could achieve the same health outcomes at 20-30% lower costs. Key reforms to improve efficiency include enhancing preventive care, restructuring the hospital system, and increasing the use of generic drugs. These reforms would free up resources that could be redirected toward meeting the needs of an aging population, particularly in long-term care.

Tax Policy Adjustments:

The recommendations for tax reforms in Belgium focus on enhancing the efficiency, fairness, and sustainability of the tax system. Belgium's fiscal challenges necessitate a series of tax adjustments aimed at reducing the tax burden on labor, improving tax collection, and addressing distortions in the current tax structure.

Reducing Labor Taxes: there is a clear need to reduce taxes on labor, a measure that could enhance labor force participation, particularly in light of Belgium's aging population and the challenges of a tight labor market. Belgium has one of the highest labor tax burdens in the OECD, which contributes to work disincentives. Reducing personal income taxes, especially at lower and middle income levels, could help to increase disposable income and incentivize greater participation in the workforce. This adjustment should also include aligning tax brackets and social benefits to avoid penalizing workers who take on additional hours or income, particularly for low-income households.

Addressing VAT Inefficiencies: Belgium's VAT system is marked by a complex structure with multiple reduced rates, which creates inefficiencies and complicates tax compliance. Gradually reducing these rate differentials, aligning them with best practices in other advanced economies, and simplifying the VAT framework is imperative. Such reforms could reduce distortions, improve transparency, and create a more neutral tax system. However, it is of critical importance to cushion the impact of VAT reform on low-income households, which would require targeted social transfers or compensatory measures.

Harmonizing Capital Taxation: The tax treatment of capital income, including property taxes and capital gains, is another area for reform. Belgium's tax system currently applies disparate rates to different types of capital income, with relatively low taxation of real estate and certain financial assets. Harmonizing the tax rates across these income sources to create a more consistent and fair system. This would not only enhance revenue generation but also help reduce incentives for tax avoidance and contribute to a more efficient allocation of resources. Additionally, improving the tax treatment of capital gains, particularly in the real estate sector, could prevent the buildup of financial imbalances and speculative bubbles.

Strengthening Tax Administration and Compliance: Belgium's tax administration is generally well-established, utilizing mechanisms such as withholding taxes to secure revenue efficiently. However, there are areas for improvement. The IMF's analysis, including an assessment using the Tax Administration Diagnostic Assessment Tool (TADAT), suggests that Belgium could enhance compliance by improving vigilance in monitoring on-time filing and payments, particularly from business taxpayers. A targeted compliance improvement plan, especially for sectors with high informal activity, such as professional services, could help reduce the VAT compliance gap, which is estimated at around 2% of GDP. Strengthening the enforcement of tax regulations and improving the transparency of tax collection would improve public trust and bolster overall fiscal revenues.

In conclusion, a comprehensive tax reform strategy that focuses on reducing labor taxes, simplifying VAT, harmonizing capital taxation, and improving compliance to create a more equitable and efficient tax system in Belgium. These measures would not only help in fiscal consolidation but also support economic growth and social equity.

These reform priorities are critical for ensuring Belgium's fiscal health and sustainability in the long term. By addressing inefficiencies in public spending and implementing more targeted, sustainable reforms, Belgium can restore fiscal stability while safeguarding its social welfare system.

Green Transition: A Pillar of Future Growth

Belgium is firmly committed to its climate transition agenda, aiming for climate neutrality by 2050. While the transition presents significant challenges, it also offers investors fertile ground for growth, particularly in green infrastructure, renewable energy, and sustainable mobility. The country's ambitious targets are complemented by EU-backed funding and policy frameworks, creating a robust environment for long-term green investments.

Targets and Challenges

Belgium has committed to achieving climate neutrality by 2050, but it faces a significant gap in meeting its interim climate goals. For instance, the country is behind in its 2030 target to reduce emissions by 32% compared to 2005 levels. Key barriers to reaching these targets include aging infrastructure, fragmented regional policies, and a high dependency on energy imports, which necessitate coordinated and ambitious action at both federal and regional levels. Addressing these challenges will require substantial investments in renewable energy, energy efficiency, and green infrastructure, which offer both environmental benefits and attractive financial returns. The gradual phase-out of fossil fuel subsidies, the implementation of carbon taxes, and increased investments in green technologies are expected to be central to overcoming these obstacles.

Opportunities for Investment

Renewable Energy: The Belgian government has set clear goals to expand renewable energy as part of its climate strategy. Offshore wind, solar power, and energy storage projects are central to these plans, presenting substantial opportunities for investment. Belgium has already made significant progress in offshore wind energy, with projects underway in the North Sea. The country's favorable geographical location, robust wind resources, and EU-wide green energy commitments make it an ideal hub for expanding these renewable energy sources. The REPowerEU initiative and the European Green Deal will likely further accelerate investment in this area, providing both public and private sector opportunities. Investors in the renewable energy sector will benefit from the growing demand for low-carbon solutions, supported by government incentives and EU funds.

Sustainable Mobility: As part of its green transition, Belgium is focusing on sustainable mobility. The country is

committed to increasing the adoption of electric vehicles
(EVs), expanding charging infrastructure, and promoting
green public transport. The transition to EVs and
electrification of transport systems is expected to grow as
Belgium works toward a carbon-neutral transport sector.
Investment in EV charging networks, especially in
underdeveloped areas and urban centers, is set to see strong
demand, creating opportunities for both infrastructure
development and service provision. Additionally, the
government's investment in green public transport, including
electric buses and trams, aligns with EU green policies and
presents long-term investment avenues.

Energy Efficiency: Retrofitting buildings and industrial
facilities for improved energy efficiency is another key focus
of Belgium's green transition. If Belgium's energy spending
matched the efficiency levels of the OECD average, it could
achieve the same healthy life expectancy at a 20-30% lower
cost. With a significant portion of the country's buildings and
industries requiring upgrades to meet climate goals, this area
is poised for substantial growth. Investments in energy-
efficient technologies, such as better insulation, advanced
heating and cooling systems, and energy-efficient industrial
equipment, will be crucial. This sector is supported by both
national and EU-level initiatives, including EU grants under
the REPowerEU program, which provides financial backing
for energy transition projects.

Coordination and Regional Challenges

One of the key challenges for investors is the fragmented
nature of Belgium's energy and climate policy. The country's

federal and regional governments have often struggled to align their policies, creating regulatory complexities that may affect investment decisions. A coordinated approach across all levels of government is essential to streamline energy policy, facilitate the smooth implementation of green projects, and maximize the impact of EU funding. However, the ongoing commitment to climate neutrality and the increasing emphasis on green investments within the EU's policy framework provide strong incentives for investors to navigate these complexities.

Belgium's green transition represents both a challenge and an opportunity for investors. While the country faces hurdles in meeting its climate targets, it is positioned to be a leader in renewable energy, sustainable mobility, and energy efficiency. Strategic investments in these sectors, supported by EU recovery funds and national initiatives, offer significant growth potential. As Belgium advances its green agenda, aligning investments with the country's climate goals will not only contribute to environmental sustainability but also yield attractive returns over the long term

Investment Climate and Sectoral Opportunities

Belgium continues to be a highly attractive destination for both domestic and foreign investments, offering a favorable business environment supported by a well-developed financial system, a strategic location at the heart of Europe, and its membership in the European Union (EU). Despite the fiscal challenges, several sectors in Belgium offer substantial growth and innovation potential. These sectors are positioned to drive both domestic development and international collaboration, particularly as the country seeks to boost productivity and competitiveness.

Information & Communication Technology (ICT) and Digital Services

Belgium boasts a robust and rapidly expanding digital infrastructure, including extensive 5G networks, which position the country as a regional hub for digital services such as fintech, cybersecurity, and data analytics. The ongoing digital transformation across industries opens new avenues for investment, especially in cloud computing, artificial intelligence (AI), and blockchain technologies. The government's focus on improving digital preparedness and innovation, as seen in its National Recovery and Resilience Plan, further underscores Belgium's role as a key player in the European digital economy. Moreover, Belgium's integration into the EU's Digital Single Market offers both opportunities and challenges for growth, with regulations that can help streamline digital services across borders.

Life Sciences and Healthcare

Belgium's biopharmaceutical industry is globally recognized for its research and development capabilities, particularly in areas like vaccines, biologics, and personalized medicine. The country's investment in life sciences is expected to continue to grow, bolstered by its strong network of universities, research institutions, and private sector collaboration. As part of the EU's Horizon Europe program, Belgium benefits from significant funding opportunities that are attracting global biotech firms. Belgium's healthcare system, though highly efficient, faces pressure due to an aging population, creating additional opportunities for investment in long-term care, medical technologies, and innovative healthcare solutions, particularly in the fields of telemedicine and digital health.

Advanced Manufacturing

Belgium's manufacturing sector is a key pillar of the economy, with a particular focus on high-tech and sustainable industries. The country is well-positioned to meet EU industrial goals, including carbon-neutral manufacturing processes, advanced materials, and automation. Sectors such as robotics, aerospace, automotive, and 3D printing stand to benefit from Belgium's investment in technology and infrastructure. As part of the EU's industrial strategy, Belgium has been supporting the green transformation of industries, particularly through the adoption of cleaner technologies in energy-intensive sectors like chemicals and steel production. Additionally, Belgium's strategic location and well-established logistics network make it an ideal base for industries focused on the EU market.

Green Finance

Belgium is positioning itself as a leader in green finance, with a growing market for green bonds and climate-aligned investments. The Belgian government has taken steps to incentivize private investment in sustainable projects, particularly in renewable energy, energy efficiency, and climate adaptation. The country's evolving green bond market is helping to provide liquidity and attractive returns for investors focused on environmental, social, and governance (ESG) criteria. Moreover, Belgium's commitment to climate neutrality by 2050 is driving demand for sustainable infrastructure projects, offering long-term investment opportunities for both domestic and international stakeholders.

Infrastructure Development: Strategic Investments in Infrastructure

Belgium's infrastructure development is essential to enhancing regional competitiveness, with a focus on transport, urban development, and cross-border energy interconnectivity. Major infrastructure projects such as the Euroconnector electricity link are pivotal in improving Belgium's energy security and supporting the EU's green transition. Additionally, investments in high-speed rail, urban mobility, and smart city technologies are being prioritized to enhance connectivity and sustainability. Belgium's strategic location as a transport and logistics hub in Europe is complemented by its extensive multimodal transport networks, which include ports, rail, and highways, facilitating efficient trade and investment flows.

Belgium's investment climate remains robust, with significant opportunities in high-tech industries, green finance, and healthcare. The government's ongoing reforms and focus on digitalization and sustainability are expected to foster growth, innovation, and international collaboration in these sectors, making Belgium an increasingly attractive destination for investors.

Key Messages for Investors: Opportunities, Risks, and Strategic Approaches

Belgium offers a complex but promising investment environment. While there are significant opportunities in various sectors, potential investors must also consider the risks and challenges that could affect returns. The IMF highlights key areas of both risk and opportunity, offering insights into how investors can navigate the evolving landscape.

Risks and Challenges for Investors

Political Fragmentation:

Belgium's political system is characterized by complex governance structures, including multiple regional governments. While this decentralization has benefits, it also creates challenges for policy implementation. The political fragmentation could delay crucial reforms, especially as the country heads into elections in 2024. This uncertainty may lead to prolonged government formation processes and slow the pace of fiscal and structural reforms. Such delays can increase risk premiums and hinder the country's ability to make timely decisions on fiscal consolidation and investments in infrastructure or the green transition .

High Labor Costs:

Belgium's labor market is under pressure from automatic wage indexation, which is designed to protect purchasing power but also increases labor costs, particularly in export-oriented sectors. This can erode Belgium's competitiveness relative to other EU countries with more flexible wage mechanisms. High labor costs may affect profitability in

sectors reliant on cost-efficient production, such as
manufacturing and logistics, which are key industries for
foreign investment .

Real Estate Cooling:

The real estate market, while traditionally a stable investment
avenue, has shown signs of cooling due to tightening
financial conditions, including rising interest rates and lower
demand in certain sectors. Belgium's exposure to the
commercial real estate sector is particularly high, making it
susceptible to risks associated with market fluctuations.
Vulnerabilities in commercial real estate lending, particularly
if economic conditions worsen is an area of concern.
Investors should monitor this sector closely, especially in
light of ongoing market adjustments and structural changes
in real estate use, such as the shift toward remote work.

A Strategic Approach for Investors

Despite these challenges, Belgium remains a strong
investment destination, especially for those focusing on
green and digital transitions. Investors should align their
strategies with Belgium's long-term goals and take advantage
of available EU funds and reforms aimed at boosting
economic resilience.

Focus on Green and Digital Transformations

As Belgium continues its transition to a greener and more
digital economy, investors should prioritize sectors aligned
with these transformations. Projects supporting climate
goals, such as renewable energy and energy efficiency,
present long-term growth potential. The country's evolving

green finance market, including green bonds and sustainable investments, offers opportunities for ESG-focused investors. Additionally, Belgium's digital transformation, particularly in fintech, cybersecurity, and data analytics, provides numerous avenues for growth. With robust digital infrastructure and EU support for green and digital initiatives, these sectors are expected to attract continued investment.

Leverage EU Recovery Funds

Belgium benefits from the EU's Recovery and Resilience Facility, which offers substantial funding for green and digital investments. This funding is part of a broader EU initiative to support economic recovery and long-term sustainability across member states. Investors should explore opportunities within Belgium's recovery and resilience plan, particularly those focused on innovation, infrastructure, and the green economy. With approximately 51% of Belgium's allocated funds earmarked for climate-related initiatives, the country is well-positioned to attract investments in clean technologies and low-carbon solutions.

Forge Local Partnerships

Given Belgium's complex regulatory environment, particularly in relation to its federal and regional governance structures, investors can benefit from forming local partnerships. Collaborating with Belgian entities can help navigate these regulatory complexities, improve market access, and mitigate risks. Local partnerships also provide valuable insights into Belgium's evolving economic policies and the political landscape.

Monitor Fiscal and Structural Reforms

Belgium's fiscal consolidation efforts, alongside ongoing reforms in the labor market, healthcare, and pension systems, will play a significant role in shaping the country's investment climate. Investors should stay informed about the government's progress on these reforms, as they are crucial for maintaining fiscal stability and ensuring long-term sustainability. Key reforms include efforts to rationalize spending, increase efficiency in social benefits, and improve the tax system. Additionally, pension reforms aimed at ensuring sustainability in the face of an aging population and healthcare reforms to increase efficiency are likely to influence both public spending and private sector opportunities.

Belgium presents a dynamic investment landscape with both risks and opportunities. A strategic focus on sectors aligned with green and digital transitions, leveraging EU recovery funds, and navigating the political and fiscal landscape with local partnerships will be key to achieving successful outcomes. By staying informed and adaptable, investors can take advantage of Belgium's strengths while managing potential challenges effectively.

Belgium: a unique blend of resilience challenges and significant potential for growth

Belgium's economic trajectory is shaped by a unique blend of resilience, challenges, and significant potential for growth.

The country's response to recent crises demonstrates its capacity to navigate turbulent times, yet the road ahead remains marked by persistent fiscal, structural, and political hurdles. As Belgium grapples with high debt, inflation pressures, and the complexities of its multi-level governance system, it also stands poised to capitalize on key opportunities that promise long-term economic transformation.

For investors, Belgium offers a compelling landscape, especially in the green and digital sectors. The country's commitment to climate neutrality by 2050, supported by EU-backed funding and initiatives, positions it as a leader in renewable energy, energy efficiency, and sustainable mobility. Additionally, the burgeoning digital economy, fueled by advances in ICT, fintech, and cybersecurity, provides a rich array of investment prospects. However, navigating this landscape requires a strategic approach, with a focus on sectors aligned with Belgium's green and digital goals, leveraging EU recovery funds, and fostering local partnerships to navigate the complexities of the country's political and regulatory environment.

Belgium's fiscal and structural reforms will play a critical role in shaping the investment climate in the coming years. The ongoing adjustments in tax policy, pension systems, and healthcare will likely impact both public spending and private sector opportunities, offering avenues for those prepared to stay informed and agile. While the challenges are notable, Belgium's strengths—its strategic location, highly skilled workforce, and robust infrastructure—remain key assets for investors. By aligning their strategies with Belgium's transformation agenda, investors can contribute to and benefit from the country's evolving economic landscape.

In conclusion, Belgium stands at a crossroads, where strategic investments in key sectors can unlock significant growth and innovation. With careful attention to the evolving policy landscape and a focus on long-term, sustainable opportunities, investors can navigate the risks and seize the potential of this transformative economy.

Chapter (8)

Sweden: Navigating the Road to Sustainable Growth Amid Complex Economic Challenges

Sweden, located in Northern Europe, has a population of around 10.5 million people and spans an area of 450,295 square kilometres. The country's economy is projected to grow at a modest 0.2% in 2024, recovering from a slight contraction of 0.3% in 2023. The nominal GDP for Sweden in FY24 is expected to reach approximately SEK 5.8 trillion.

Sweden, with its reputation as a stable and innovative economy, is at a pivotal point in its journey. The country, known for its strong institutions, comprehensive social safety nets, and advanced technological sector, now faces a series of challenges and opportunities. After a remarkable post-pandemic recovery, Sweden's economic growth has softened, as the global economic environment shifts and domestic pressures mount. This chapter explores Sweden's current economic trajectory, its fiscal and monetary policy frameworks, as well as the evolving landscape for investment, the regulatory environment, and the structural reforms required to sustain long-term prosperity.

Economic Performance: Resilience in the Face of Global Uncertainty

Economic Trajectory: Slowing Growth, Steadying Foundations

Sweden's economic performance has been nothing short of resilient. After an exceptional recovery from the pandemic, the economy saw a notable slowdown in 2023. A contraction of 0.3% in GDP marked the beginning of a more subdued phase, as weak private consumption and declining residential investment took their toll on the economy. Despite this, the outlook for 2024 remains cautiously optimistic. Growth is projected to be a modest 0.2% in 2024, but there is light at the end of the tunnel, as Sweden's economic dynamism is expected to resurface, with growth gradually accelerating to 2.3% by 2025.

Sweden's performance is deeply intertwined with global economic trends. As an export-oriented economy, fluctuations in global demand—particularly from key markets such as Germany, Norway, and the Netherlands—have a significant impact on its domestic economic health. In 2023, external pressures, such as tighter financial conditions, high energy prices, and weakening international trade, constrained Sweden's domestic consumption. These challenges are expected to continue into 2024, but with a more stable global outlook, Sweden's economy is poised to recover, driven by stronger private consumption as inflation eases.

Inflation and Labor Market Adjustments: Navigating Tightening Conditions

Inflation, which had surged to 10.8% by the end of 2022, has begun to subside. By the end of 2023, the inflation rate had decreased significantly to 1.9%, primarily due to a drop in energy prices. This disinflationary trend has offered a much-needed reprieve for households that were grappling with eroding real incomes. However, core inflation, which remains stubbornly high at 5.3%, poses ongoing challenges for the Swedish economy. The gradual return to the Riksbank's inflation target of 2% by mid-2025 is a top priority for policymakers, who are balancing the needs of a cooling labor market with efforts to maintain financial stability.

The Swedish labor market, once a pillar of strong growth, has shown signs of cooling. The unemployment rate, which had been historically low, ticked up to 8% by the end of 2023. While still modest compared to global averages, this uptick reflects a broader trend of slowed employment growth, which decelerated from 3% in 2022 to 1.4% in 2023. Wage growth has also moderated, settling at around 4% annually. These trends reflect the combined effects of restrictive monetary policies and slower economic activity.

Despite these adjustments, Sweden's labor market remains one of the most resilient in Europe, with relatively low unemployment and a highly skilled workforce. However, the cooling labor market presents challenges that need to be addressed through structural reforms, particularly to match skills with the evolving needs of a green and digital economy.

Fiscal Policy: Navigating Pressures and Investing in the Future

Managing Deficits and Public Debt: A Strong Foundation for Fiscal Flexibility

Sweden's fiscal policy framework has proven to be a key strength during these turbulent times. The government's decision to adopt a broadly neutral fiscal stance in 2024, with a slight widening of the fiscal deficit to 0.7% of GDP, is a pragmatic approach to navigate the economic slowdown while avoiding inflationary pressures. This fiscal prudence is underpinned by Sweden's robust public finances, which have been carefully managed to provide substantial fiscal space for the future.

In 2023, despite the economic headwinds, Sweden's fiscal deficit remained under control, largely thanks to prudent expenditure management. With substantial fiscal space available, Sweden is well-positioned to deploy targeted fiscal support if needed, particularly for vulnerable populations affected by the high cost of living and rising debt-servicing burdens.

However, the medium-term challenges are clear. Sweden must tackle rising public spending pressures, particularly in healthcare, pensions, and social services, exacerbated by demographic shifts. There is also an urgent need for public investment to support the green transition, as Sweden accelerates its efforts to meet its ambitious climate goals. As the government looks toward the coming decades, it will need to balance fiscal prudence with the need to make substantial investments in infrastructure, innovation, and social resilience.

Tax Reforms: Shaping the Future of Sweden's Fiscal Landscape

Tax reforms are high on the agenda for Sweden, particularly given the need to rationalize dividend taxation, reduce the tax burden on labor income, and improve property taxation. It is suggested that Sweden should focus on lowering labor income taxes to reduce the large labor tax wedge, which currently acts as a deterrent for both skilled foreign workers and domestic business expansion.

The Swedish government is also examining ways to improve property taxation to support a more efficient and equitable tax system. In addition to these tax reforms, Sweden has signaled a commitment to addressing the tax deductibility of interest payments, which currently distorts investment incentives and contributes to excessive leverage in the real estate sector. These reforms, along with a shift toward taxation that incentivizes green investments, will be crucial in ensuring that Sweden's fiscal policy remains both sustainable and growth-enhancing.

Investment Opportunities: Harnessing the Green Transition and Digital Innovation

Green Economy: Sweden's Path to a Sustainable Future

Sweden's commitment to a sustainable future is exemplified by its ambitious goal of achieving net-zero emissions by 2045. To meet this target, the government is channelling investments into green technologies, renewable energy infrastructure, and carbon capture initiatives. The discovery of a significant rare-earth deposit in Northern Sweden, which is crucial for electrification and battery production, offers a unique opportunity to accelerate Sweden's green transition. This deposit positions Sweden as a critical player in Europe's shift towards clean energy and electrification, providing fertile ground for green investments.

The green economy presents a wealth of opportunities for investors. Sweden is investing heavily in renewable energy sources such as wind, solar, and hydropower, with plans to increase the share of renewables in its energy mix. The country is also working on scaling up green infrastructure, including electric vehicle charging networks and sustainable building initiatives. For investors, Sweden offers not only a stable political and economic environment but also a forward-thinking approach to sustainability that aligns with the global shift towards decarbonization.

Digital Transformation: Fueling Innovation and Growth

Sweden is at the forefront of digital innovation, particularly in areas such as artificial intelligence (AI), fintech, and smart manufacturing. The government's focus on digital transformation is driving investments in new technologies and digital infrastructure. Sweden's highly educated workforce, combined with its vibrant startup ecosystem, makes it an attractive destination for venture capital and private equity investments in emerging sectors like fintech, AI, and blockchain technology.

Sweden is also a leader in integrating digitalization with sustainability. The growing demand for digital solutions to tackle climate challenges presents a unique opportunity for investors to tap into the intersection of technology and sustainability. The country's forward-looking regulatory environment, combined with its commitment to fostering innovation, positions Sweden as a hub for investment in the digital economy.

Structural Reforms: Ensuring Inclusive and Sustainable Growth

Labor Market Reforms: Addressing Skills Mismatches and Labor Mobility

One of Sweden's most pressing challenges is the need to address structural unemployment and skills mismatches. Despite its strong workforce, Sweden faces high unemployment among certain demographics, particularly young people, immigrants, and low-skilled workers. To tackle this, the Swedish government has launched initiatives such as the "work first" principle, aimed at improving employability through tailored training and mentorship programs. These efforts are designed to enhance labor mobility and ensure that the workforce is prepared for the digital and green transformation of the economy.

Education and upskilling will be critical to ensuring that Sweden's labor force remains competitive. There is a vital need for continuous investment in education and training programs, particularly in digital skills, to equip workers for the rapidly changing labor market. Sweden's emphasis on reskilling through programs such as the Study Grant for Transition is a step in the right direction, ensuring that workers can adapt to new technologies and job opportunities.

Housing Market Reforms: Creating a More Dynamic and Flexible Economy

Sweden's housing market remains one of the most significant barriers to economic mobility and growth. The high cost of housing, coupled with stringent building regulations and rent controls, has created a bottleneck that limits the supply of affordable housing and impedes labor mobility. Addressing these challenges requires comprehensive reforms, including easing rent controls, simplifying building codes, and increasing the supply of land for construction.

The government has committed to streamlining building regulations and planning procedures to make it easier to build new housing. These changes are essential not only for addressing the housing shortage but also for enabling Sweden to attract and retain talent from across Europe and the world. By reducing the regulatory burden on construction, Sweden can create a more flexible and dynamic housing market, which will help foster a more mobile and productive workforce.

Conclusion: A Forward-Thinking Sweden Poised for a Sustainable Future

Sweden stands at a crossroads in its economic journey. While the country faces challenges in terms of slowing growth, rising inflation, and labor market pressures, its strong institutional framework, commitment to sustainability, and technological innovation provide a solid foundation for future growth. Sweden's ongoing fiscal and monetary policy adjustments, coupled with structural reforms in the labor market, housing, and taxation, will be crucial in ensuring the country remains competitive on the global stage.

For investors, Sweden offers significant opportunities in green technologies, digital innovation, and sustainable infrastructure. With its focus on climate adaptation, renewable energy, and digital transformation, Sweden is poised to lead the charge in Europe's green and digital revolutions. Through strategic investments, continued innovation, and forward-thinking policies, Sweden is well-positioned to achieve long-term sustainable growth and prosperity, making it an attractive destination for those seeking stability, innovation, and growth in the years ahead.

Chapter (9)

Ireland: Charting a Path Through Opportunities and Challenges for Sustainable Economic Growth

Ireland is an island nation located in the North Atlantic, sharing a border with Northern Ireland (a part of the United Kingdom). The country has a population of approximately 5.2 million people and is known for its dynamic economy, which is heavily influenced by foreign direct investment (FDI) and multinational corporations. In FY24, Ireland's GDP is projected to grow by 2.7%, reaching a nominal GDP of €575.1 billion, driven by strong exports and domestic consumption.

Ireland stands as a global economic exemplar, demonstrating resilience amid successive external shocks, structural bottlenecks, and evolving fiscal dynamics. This chapter delves into Ireland's economic landscape, leveraging insights from the 2023 IMF Article IV consultation, with a focus on growth trajectories, fiscal policies, tax reforms, and investment opportunities. A deeper understanding of key metrics, such as Modified Gross National Income (GNI), allows for a nuanced view of Ireland's economy beyond the influence of multinational enterprises (MNEs).

Economic Performance: Stability in a Globalized Economy

Understanding GNI and GNI

Gross National Income (GNI) measures the total income earned by a country's residents, including income generated abroad, but excludes income paid to non-residents. Ireland uses *Modified GNI (GNI)* to better reflect its domestic economy by excluding MNE activities, such as depreciation of intellectual property and leased aircraft, and net factor income of redomiciled companies. This adjustment is crucial in Ireland's context, where MNE operations significantly inflate traditional GDP figures, providing a misleading picture of domestic economic performance.

Economic Growth Amidst Global Challenges

Ireland's economy remains robust, driven by strong private consumption and a gradual recovery in real income as inflation moderates. Real GNI* is forecasted to grow at 2.5% in 2023–2024 before stabilizing at a potential rate of 2.25%. While Modified Domestic Demand (MDD) rebounded in mid-2023, risks from supply-side constraints, notably housing shortages and labor market mismatches, weigh on sustained growth. Additionally, external headwinds, such as geopolitical uncertainties and weaker global demand for pharmaceutical and technology exports, highlight the economy's vulnerability as a highly open system.

Inflation and Labor Market Dynamics

Inflation peaked at 9.6% in mid-2022 but declined to 3.6% by October 2023, supported by falling energy prices and easing supply chain pressures. Core inflation, driven by services and processed food costs, remains a concern at 4.6%, reflecting broader economic tightness. The unemployment rate, at 4.8% as of late 2023, signals a tight labor market despite marginal easing, with construction and high-skill sectors experiencing acute labor shortages. Wage growth at 5.1% is just shy of inflation, signaling improving real incomes but limited scope for a significant consumption surge.

Fiscal Policy: Building Buffers Amid Uncertainty

Public Debt and Deficit Dynamics

Ireland's fiscal position remains strong, with a surplus of 1.7% of GDP in 2022 and public debt on a declining trajectory, down to 44% of GDP. However, when measured against GNI, public debt remains relatively high at 82%, underscoring vulnerabilities from concentrated revenue streams. Corporate Income Tax (CIT) revenues, heavily reliant on top-performing MNEs in technology and pharmaceuticals, constitute a precarious fiscal pillar. Excess CIT revenues—estimated at €12 billion in 2022—should be considered transitory and saved in designated funds to mitigate volatility.

Tax Reform and Revenue Diversification

It is essential to broaden and diversify Ireland's tax base to enhance fiscal resilience. Recommendations include:

Personal Income Tax (PIT): Introducing additional bands and rates to enhance progressivity while broadening the base.

Value-Added Tax (VAT): Simplifying exemptions to improve compliance while retaining administrative efficiency.

Corporate Taxation: Avoiding permanent spending tied to volatile CIT revenues and aligning fiscal incentives with sustainability goals.

Property Taxes: Expanding this stable revenue source to fund long-term investment needs.

Ireland's medium-term fiscal policy aligns with these goals, focusing on public investment while safeguarding sustainability.

Investment Landscape: Opportunities and Challenges

Addressing Housing and Infrastructure Bottlenecks

Ireland's housing market faces acute supply shortages, with residential property prices declining marginally in 2023 after years of steep increases. Structural issues, including low productivity in construction, labor shortages, and regulatory delays, exacerbate the housing gap. Policies to boost supply include streamlining planning processes, increasing housing

density, and replacing rent caps with targeted support for
vulnerable households. These efforts aim to align supply with
rising demand fueled by population growth, immigration,
and economic expansion.

Public investment under the National Development Plan
(NDP) is critical for addressing infrastructure gaps, including
transport, housing, and renewable energy. However,
execution risks persist, as capacity constraints in the
construction sector may delay project timelines and inflate
costs.

Green Transition and Innovation

Ireland's commitment to the green transition presents
lucrative opportunities in renewable energy, energy-efficient
infrastructure, and electric grid modernization. Achieving
carbon neutrality by 2050 will require sustained investment
in these areas, supported by climate-focused fiscal policies.
Digital innovation also offers growth potential, particularly
through initiatives that enhance the competitiveness of small
and medium-sized enterprises (SMEs) via R&D support and
partnerships with MNEs.

Strategic Outlook: Ensuring Resilience Through Reform

Managing Fiscal and Financial Risks

Ireland's financial ecosystem, including banks and non-bank
financial institutions (NBFIs), remains robust but faces
vulnerabilities from tighter global financial conditions. The
commercial real estate (CRE) sector, under pressure from

declining valuations and rising vacancy rates, poses potential spillovers to financial stability. Prudential measures, such as increased counter-cyclical capital buffers (CCyB) and macroprudential oversight, are critical to safeguarding resilience.

Structural Reforms for Sustainable Growth

Ireland's ability to navigate external and domestic challenges hinges on strategic reforms, including:

Taxation: Saving excess CIT revenues in sovereign funds to buffer against shocks.

Housing: Enhancing construction sector efficiency and expediting planning approvals.

Digital and Green Economies: Supporting SMEs through digital transformation and fostering industrial clusters for innovation.

Education and Skills: Addressing labor market mismatches through targeted investments in STEM education and vocational training.

Chapter conclusion: Ireland a blend of opportunities amidst complexities

Ireland's economic landscape, shaped by globalization and domestic challenges, offers a blend of opportunities and complexities. Prudent fiscal management, targeted investments, and comprehensive reforms will be essential for sustaining inclusive growth. For investors, Ireland presents a dynamic environment characterized by robust domestic demand, cutting-edge innovation, and a strong commitment to sustainability. However, navigating regulatory and fiscal intricacies will be crucial in realizing the country's long-term economic potential.

Chapter (10)

Austria: A Strategic Economic and Investment Landscape Amidst Transition

Austria, located in Central Europe, covers an area of approximately 83,879 square kilometres and has a population of around 9.1 million people as of 2024. The country's economy, characterized by high levels of industrialization and services, has shown resilience in the face of recent challenges, including the pandemic and the energy crisis exacerbated by geopolitical tensions. Austria's GDP is projected to reach about $541 billion in 2024, with a per capita GDP of approximately $56,726.

Austria, a country known for its economic resilience and robust social systems, is navigating through an evolving economic environment marked by post-pandemic recovery, fiscal reforms, inflationary pressures, and the imperative to meet ambitious green transition goals. The IMF's 2024 Article IV Consultation report sheds light on Austria's economic and fiscal trajectory, offering insights into the country's growth prospects, fiscal sustainability, and strategic investment sectors. As Austria faces both challenges and opportunities, understanding its current economic landscape

and key policy directions is essential for investors looking for
stable yet dynamic growth prospects.

Economic Recovery and Inflation Dynamics

Austria's economy demonstrated impressive recovery from
the pandemic's initial shock, returning to pre-pandemic
output levels by 2022. However, in 2023, a combination of
high energy prices, inflationary pressures, and elevated
interest rates resulted in a contraction of 0.8% in GDP.
Despite this downturn, Austria's economy is poised for a
modest recovery in 2024, underpinned by private
consumption driven by rising real wages. Key aspects
shaping the economic outlook include inflation, labor market
developments, and the broader macroeconomic
environment.

Inflation Trajectory: A Gradual Decline

Austria's inflation has been persistently higher than the euro-
area average, with core inflation proving particularly sticky
due to rapid wage growth in the services sector. The sharp
spike in inflation to nearly 12% in early 2023 was driven by
soaring energy prices exacerbated by the geopolitical tensions
surrounding Russia's invasion of Ukraine. Since then,
inflation has gradually moderated, with energy prices
stabilizing, but core inflation has remained above 4% as
services, particularly in tourism and hospitality, continued to
experience upward price pressures.

Inflation Projections: A gradual reduction in inflation is
anticipated, with headline inflation expected to ease to
around 4.0% in 2024, eventually reaching the European

Central Bank's 2% target by the second half of 2025. However, the persistence of high services sector inflation means that Austria may not see a full return to price stability for some time. Investors should be mindful of inflation risks in sectors with sticky price levels, especially in consumer services and real estate.

Labor Market Resilience Amidst Economic Contraction

Despite economic contraction, Austria's labor market remains resilient, reflecting tight employment conditions and significant wage growth. In 2023, Austria's employment rate reached record highs, and wages grew faster than the euro-area average. However, the economic slowdown has led to a slight increase in unemployment and a decrease in vacancy rates. Structural shifts are also visible, particularly in the growing share of part-time employment, reflecting evolving work preferences.

Key Labor Market Trends: The trend toward more part-time and flexible work arrangements, particularly among women, reflects broader societal changes. There is an essential need for continued labor market reforms to address demographic pressures, such as increasing the labor participation rate of elderly workers and closing gender wage gaps. The shift towards part-time employment and a reduction in total hours worked suggest potential challenges in labor productivity and economic growth, particularly as Austria faces an aging population.

Fiscal Policies: Balancing Sustainability with Strategic Investments

Austria's fiscal policy has played a critical role in mitigating recent economic shocks, but significant challenges remain. While the fiscal deficit narrowed slightly to 2.7% of GDP in 2023, fiscal pressures are mounting due to demographic trends, rising healthcare costs, and defense spending needs. Continued fiscal consolidation to stabilize public debt while ensuring sufficient room for strategic investments, particularly in green infrastructure is imperative.

Public Debt and Deficit: Managing Long-Term Sustainability

Austria's public debt ratio, while still relatively low compared to other European nations, increased to 77.7% of GDP in 2023, largely due to pandemic-related spending and energy-price support measures. A gradual reduction in the debt-to-GDP ratio over the medium term is projected, but demographic factors, including the aging population and rising social welfare costs, are expected to exert upward pressure on public spending.

Fiscal Deficit Reduction: A cautious approach to deficit reduction, suggesting a moderate fiscal tightening of 0.3% of GDP annually through 2028 to bring the structural primary balance close to zero by 2028. This would stabilize the public debt at sustainable levels and allow room for investment in green infrastructure and other critical areas. The government has already begun phasing out energy subsidies, which will help reduce the fiscal deficit, though higher public investment in climate initiatives and defense could offset these savings.

Green Transition Investment Needs

Austria is committed to achieving a 48% reduction in non-ETS emissions by 2030, but the current trajectory falls short of this target. The country has made progress in integrating renewable energy sources, but regulatory delays in green project approvals and skill shortages in key sectors pose significant challenges.

Investment Opportunities in Green Infrastructure: Accelerating the green transition will require substantial public investment in renewable energy infrastructure, energy efficiency, and green technologies. Public-private partnerships, particularly in the energy sector, offer significant opportunities for investors in clean energy, energy storage solutions, and sustainable urban infrastructure.

Inflation and Monetary Policy: Adjusting to Changing Conditions

Austria continues to grapple with inflation dynamics shaped by a complex interplay of global and domestic factors. The gradual decline in inflation observed since its peak in early 2023 underscores the challenges in addressing both supply-driven and demand-driven components. Sticky services inflation, buoyed by robust wage growth and the lingering effects of pandemic-related demand surges in tourism, hospitality, and other service sectors, remains a focal point for policymakers. The moderation of energy prices, while easing headline inflation, has not yet fully translated to core inflation metrics.

Factors Influencing Inflation Trajectory

Global Energy Prices: Despite a recent normalization in energy markets, Austria's significant reliance on imported gas, particularly from Russia, poses ongoing risks. Supply disruptions could lead to renewed inflationary pressures, particularly in energy-intensive industries.

Wage Dynamics: Elevated wage growth, surpassing Eurozone averages, has supported household consumption but also contributed to persistent core inflation. Wage agreements, which are often multi-year and indexed to inflation, indicate that this pressure may persist in the medium term.

Eurozone Economic Environment: The interconnected nature of Eurozone economies means that Austria's inflation trajectory is closely tied to broader regional trends. The European Central Bank's (ECB) policies and external demand fluctuations will significantly shape outcomes.

Monetary Policy Outlook

The European Central Bank's anticipated monetary easing in 2024–2025 presents a nuanced landscape for Austria. While easing is expected to stimulate investment, caution will be required to balance inflationary risks:

Credit Availability: Persistent inflation in Austria's services sector suggests that the ECB may adopt a measured approach, prolonging a period of cautious policy adjustments. The ability of Austrian businesses and households to access affordable credit will hinge on these policies.

Real Estate Market Dynamics: Higher interest rates have dampened mortgage lending, contributing to a cooling housing market. The ECB's policy path will be critical in determining whether these corrections stabilize or amplify broader economic risks.

Strategic Considerations for Policymakers

Monitoring Core Inflation: A clear need to address structural factors driving services inflation. Policy measures that encourage competition and productivity in high-inflation sectors could aid disinflation efforts without stifling growth.

Energy Transition and Inflation: Accelerating Austria's green transition could mitigate medium- to long-term inflation risks by reducing reliance on volatile energy imports. Investment in renewable energy and efficiency improvements in housing and transportation are highlighted as key areas.

Labor Market Policies: Enhancing labor market flexibility and addressing gender and age participation gaps can alleviate wage pressures while supporting economic growth.

In conclusion, it is important to maintain fiscal and monetary discipline in navigating these inflationary challenges. The

ECB's monetary policy adjustments, combined with
Austria's structural reforms and targeted fiscal measures, will
play a pivotal role in fostering a stable economic
environment that balances growth with price stability.

.

Investment Opportunities: Green Energy, Digital Infrastructure, and Housing

Austria's investment landscape is diverse, with significant
opportunities in sectors aligned with its long-term growth
strategy, such as green energy, digital infrastructure, and
housing. The country's green transition goals, combined with
its commitment to digitalization, make it a prime location for
strategic investments.

Green Energy Transition: A High-Value Investment Sector

Austria's ambitious environmental goals—such as achieving
net-zero emissions by 2040 and reducing emissions by 48%
by 2030—are driving investment in renewable energy and
energy efficiency. Investment in solar, wind, and energy
storage technologies is crucial to meet these targets.

Government Support for Green Initiatives: It is
paramount to remove regulatory bottlenecks and enhancing
public investment in green infrastructure. Investors in clean
energy, particularly in solar, wind, and electric vehicle
infrastructure, are likely to benefit from Austria's green
transition policies and EU-backed funding mechanisms
aimed at reducing carbon emissions.

Digitalization and Innovation: A Key Growth Driver

Austria's commitment to digitalizing its economy is another important area for investment. The country has outlined strategic plans to improve digital connectivity, particularly in rural areas, and to support the adoption of automation technologies. Investment in digital infrastructure, including 5G, AI, and cybersecurity, presents long-term opportunities for growth.

Investing in Digital Infrastructure: There is a need for continued investment in digital infrastructure to improve economic productivity and mitigate labor shortages. Investors in tech and digital infrastructure will find fertile ground in Austria as the government accelerates digital adoption across sectors.

Real Estate and Housing Market Challenges

The Austrian housing market, particularly in Vienna, faces significant affordability challenges. With real house prices increasing by 74% from 2010 to 2021, the supply of new housing has not kept up with demand. Strict regulatory controls and permitting delays have contributed to housing market bottlenecks.

Investment in Housing and Urban Development: Austria's government is taking steps to ease restrictions on new housing construction and improve housing affordability. Investment in residential real estate and urban development, particularly in Vienna and other urban centers, presents opportunities as regulatory constraints ease and new housing projects move forward.

Key Takeaways for Investors

Austria presents a promising yet multifaceted investment landscape that combines opportunities for growth with challenges requiring careful navigation. The country's robust economic fundamentals, commitment to sustainability, and emphasis on technological advancement position it as an attractive destination for long-term investments. However, investors should remain mindful of several critical considerations:

Policy-Aligned Investment Sectors

Green Technology and Renewable Energy: Austria is accelerating its green transition, supported by the European Union's Recovery and Resilience Facility and domestic climate initiatives. Investments in renewable energy infrastructure, such as solar and wind projects, are highly incentivized. The government's efforts to streamline regulatory bottlenecks in environmental permitting and promote carbon-neutral energy use provide a fertile ground for growth in this sector.

Digital Infrastructure: Austria's strategic roadmap for digitalization includes significant investments in digital infrastructure, particularly in rural connectivity and advanced technologies. EU funding underpins these initiatives, offering investors opportunities in areas like telecommunications, cybersecurity, and AI-driven solutions.

Sustainable Transportation: With ambitious emissions reduction targets, Austria is focusing on enhancing public transport and promoting electric vehicle infrastructure, offering growth prospects for investors aligned with sustainability.

Fiscal Sustainability and Structural Reforms

Fiscal Flexibility and Challenges: Austria's fiscal policies balance immediate economic support with long-term sustainability. While the country retains some fiscal space due to effective debt management, medium-term pressures such as rising pension and healthcare costs necessitate strategic reforms. Investors should monitor how these fiscal adjustments, including spending cuts and tax reforms, impact growth and funding opportunities.

Infrastructure Investments: Public and private collaboration in infrastructure, particularly in the green and digital domains, remains a priority. Strategic allocation of EU funds and the government's focus on high-impact projects enhance the potential for stable returns in infrastructure-linked investments.

Caution in Housing and Real Estate

Overvaluation and Market Risks: The housing market, especially in Vienna, faces significant overvaluation—estimated at around 30%. Declining real estate prices, tightening credit conditions, and regulatory changes aimed at curbing housing speculation pose risks for investors in this sector. Investors should focus on monitoring macroprudential policies, such as borrower-based limits on mortgage lending, which have been implemented to mitigate systemic risks.

Supply-Side Improvements: The government's push to ease land-use regulations, improve permitting processes, and incentivize affordable housing construction could gradually alleviate supply-side constraints. These developments will shape medium-term investment dynamics in residential and commercial real estate.

Broader Economic Considerations

Demographic and Labor Market Trends: Aging demographics and efforts to boost labor-force participation, especially among women and older workers, will influence Austria's economic potential. Investments in sectors benefiting from enhanced labor market participation, such as healthcare and childcare infrastructure, may yield long-term gains.

Geopolitical and Energy Security: Austria's reliance on Russian gas imports remains a vulnerability, though its high gas storage levels and diversification efforts reduce immediate risks. Energy market developments and Austria's progress in transitioning to renewables will be key factors for investors to watch.

Austria's combination of sustainability-focused policies, digital transformation initiatives, and fiscal prudence offers a dynamic investment environment. Investors aligned with the country's long-term policy goals in green energy, digital infrastructure, and sustainable housing stand to benefit from strong government and EU support. However, navigating the complexities of real estate overvaluation, fiscal adjustments, and evolving regulatory landscapes requires strategic foresight and continuous market assessment.

Austria's Path Forward: Strategic Growth Amid Challenges

As the Alpine winds of change sweep through Austria's economic and investment landscape, they carry both opportunities and challenges for those with a vision for the future. This nation, steeped in a history of resilience and innovation, now stands at the intersection of transition and transformation. Austria, a country that is striving to balance its rich heritage of fiscal prudence with the demands of a rapidly evolving global economy.

Austria's story is one of contrasts: a labor market resilient amidst contraction, a housing market under pressure yet ripe with potential, and a fiscal framework stretched yet robust. The green energy revolution pulses through its economy, lighting the way for investors in renewables and digital infrastructure, while demographic shifts and inflationary pressures test the limits of policy ingenuity.

For investors, Austria represents more than a safe harbor; it is a proving ground for sustainable growth and forward-thinking strategies. Its commitment to green technologies, digital innovation, and infrastructure modernization is not just policy—it is a call to action. Yet, as with any ascent, the climb demands caution. Navigating overvalued real estate markets, fluctuating energy dynamics, and the imperatives of fiscal sustainability requires dexterity and a keen eye on the horizon.

Austria's future, much like its storied past, is shaped by those willing to embrace its complexities and harness its promise. It offers a partnership to those who dream not only of returns but of building a legacy in a land where the old meets the new, and where tradition fuels transformation. As Austria embarks on this next chapter, it invites investors to join the journey—a journey of resilience, innovation, and growth amidst a changing world.

Bahaa G. Arnouk

Chapter (11)

Denmark: A Strategic Economic and Investment Landscape in Transition

Denmark, located in Northern Europe, covers an area of about 43,094 square kilometres. The country has a population of approximately 5.9 million in 2024. Denmark's economy has shown resilience despite facing external shocks, with its GDP projected to grow by 1.9% in FY24. The economic growth is largely driven by the pharmaceutical and maritime sectors, although the broader economy has experienced slower growth. Denmark's nominal GDP for FY24 is forecast to reach approximately $400 billion.

Denmark's economic trajectory is emblematic of a country poised at the crossroads of tradition and future-forward innovation. Historically celebrated for its stable welfare state and high standard of living, Denmark now faces the dynamic challenges of an evolving global economy—one that demands sustainability, digital transformation, and robust economic adaptation. Anchored by transparent governance, Denmark's institutions offer the backbone for a flourishing investment environment. This chapter expands upon Denmark's evolving economic landscape, leveraging insights from the IMF's 2024 Article IV consultation, which highlights critical reforms and investment opportunities shaping the country's future.

Economic Performance and Strategic Adjustments

The Danish economy, a beacon of stability amidst global uncertainties, is currently undergoing a recalibration—one that harmonizes robust industries with the imperative of future sustainability. The pharmaceutical, maritime, and renewable energy sectors remain crucial pillars, but they are now evolving to navigate the challenges of slower growth and international risks.

Economic Trajectory and Sectoral Contributions

Denmark's GDP growth, which reached 2.5% in 2023, is expected to moderate in the coming years, projected at 1.9% for 2024 and 1.6% for 2025. This anticipated slowdown reflects the normalization of previously booming sectors like pharmaceuticals and maritime, while other industries—particularly technology and renewable energy—are expected to gain ground. Denmark's commitment to sustainability, including its leadership in offshore wind, energy efficiency, and green tech, will play a decisive role in shifting the economic balance toward future-focused sectors.

Inflation and Labor Market Outlook

Inflation, which surged to an alarming 11.4% in 2022, has significantly moderated, falling to 1.8% in 2024. This reduction is due in part to Denmark's disciplined monetary policies, which have worked to stabilize prices while protecting purchasing power. Structural challenges within the labor market, particularly skill mismatches, remain prevalent, but the country is keenly focused on reforms to enhance labor market flexibility, particularly in ensuring greater participation among older workers and immigrants.

The labor market is also seeing signs of wage pressures, driven by collective agreements that, while improving living standards, could contribute to short-term price elevations. The unemployment rate, a stable 2.8% in 2023, is expected to rise modestly to 3% by 2025 as demand for labor adjusts to more moderate growth.

Fiscal Management: Preparing for Future Demands

Denmark's fiscal stewardship, long recognized as one of the most prudent in Europe, remains robust. With public debt at just 29.7% of GDP in 2023—one of the lowest ratios in advanced economies—Denmark is exceptionally positioned to navigate future demographic, climate, and defense-related spending pressures. This fiscal discipline is not just a legacy but an ongoing commitment to sustainability, with structural reforms targeting tax efficiency and reduced dependency on subsidies. The general government surplus of 3.3% of GDP in 2023 reflects Denmark's ability to reinvest in critical sectors while maintaining fiscal flexibility. However, a slight fiscal easing in 2025 is necessary to address rising expenditure demands, particularly in the areas of health and defense.

Pioneering Investment Opportunities

Denmark's regulatory environment remains a compelling invitation to international investors, particularly those with an eye on sustainability and digital innovation. The country has set ambitious goals in both the green economy and technological sectors, creating a fertile ground for investment in the years to come.

Green Economy Leadership

Denmark is a front-runner in global climate policy, with the government continuing to champion ambitious emissions reduction targets. Denmark's commitment to sustainability is reflected in its substantial investments in renewable energy infrastructure, including offshore wind farms and solar energy initiatives. Public-private partnerships, supported by progressive regulatory frameworks, are crucial to scaling these initiatives. For investors, the green transition presents significant opportunities in energy storage, wind technologies, and energy efficiency solutions. Furthermore, the reopening of the Tyra natural gas field promises near-term prospects, particularly in energy production.

Digital Transformation: Technological Innovation

The Danish government's strategic emphasis on digital transformation sets the stage for substantial growth in high-tech industries. Denmark's digital infrastructure is poised for expansion, supporting innovations in artificial intelligence, health-tech, and automation. These sectors not only promise higher productivity and competitiveness but also offer investors access to a rapidly growing market with cutting-edge capabilities in sustainability. Danish companies are leveraging digital solutions to drive sustainability goals, enhancing the potential for innovation-led growth.

Financial Resilience and Market Adjustments

Despite challenges in the global economy, Denmark's financial sector demonstrates resilience. It is noticeable that

Denmark's banks maintain robust capital buffers, with a Common Equity Tier 1 (CET1) ratio significantly above EU averages. This financial strength, combined with strong liquidity levels, ensures the stability of the country's banking system even amidst higher borrowing costs. Residential real estate shows signs of stabilization, though the commercial real estate sector faces slower recovery due to high borrowing costs, prompting macroprudential tightening.

Navigating Structural and External Risks

Denmark's highly integrated position in the global economy presents both vast opportunities and significant risks. The country's openness to trade and investment, particularly through its deep connections within global value chains, enhances its competitive edge but simultaneously exposes it to various external vulnerabilities. Denmark's economic landscape must navigate an array of risks that range from geopolitical volatility to the internal pressures of demographic changes and labor market shifts. These risks demand proactive policy measures, strategic reforms, and flexible economic management to ensure Denmark's continued resilience in a rapidly changing world.

External Risks: Geopolitical and Global Economic Vulnerabilities

Denmark's status as a highly open economy with a significant presence in global supply chains leaves it susceptible to external shocks. The ongoing geopolitical tensions—particularly from supply chain disruptions, trade restrictions, and conflicts—represent critical risks. These external factors, exacerbated by the war in Ukraine and the broader geopolitical landscape, have underscored the vulnerabilities inherent in Denmark's reliance on global trade routes and foreign investments. Denmark's strong alignment with international economic and political blocs, including its role within the EU and its membership in NATO, provides some degree of security. However, these affiliations also increase exposure to global instability, where shifts in international policy and economic conditions can have immediate and lasting effects on trade flows and supply chains.

Additionally, the IMF's report highlights how Denmark's maritime sector, crucial to its economic stability, faces significant risks from global shipping disruptions. These challenges underscore the need for Denmark to diversify its economic base to mitigate over-reliance on a few key sectors. A strategy focused on reducing vulnerability to global volatility by fostering innovation in emerging sectors like technology and renewable energy will be central to safeguarding the country's long-term economic resilience.

Demographic Pressures and Aging Population

Denmark's demographic challenges, particularly its aging population, pose a formidable challenge for sustaining economic growth and social stability. As the population continues to age, Denmark faces increasing pressures on its pension systems and healthcare services. By 2025, the country's dependency ratio will rise, meaning fewer working-age individuals will be available to support the growing number of retirees. This demographic shift necessitates urgent reforms in both the pension system and healthcare infrastructure to ensure long-term sustainability.

Simultaneously, Denmark must address the need for labor force participation among older citizens and immigrant populations, which remains crucial in maintaining economic productivity. Although Denmark has implemented policies to encourage labor market participation—particularly for older workers and those with lower educational qualifications—there is more to be done to fully integrate these groups into the workforce. Strategic investments in retraining and reskilling programs, as well as policies that support the retention of older workers, will help mitigate the demographic challenge while bolstering Denmark's productivity levels.

Sectoral Dependencies and the Need for Economic Diversification

Denmark's economic structure is notably dominated by a few key sectors—pharmaceuticals, maritime industries, and renewable energy—which, while highly successful, create a vulnerability to global economic shifts. The IMF's 2024 assessment points to the risks associated with over-reliance on these sectors, particularly given the potential for external shocks to disrupt global supply chains. While the pharmaceutical sector has proven to be resilient, external risks related to international regulations and global health challenges are unpredictable. Similarly, Denmark's maritime sector, which plays a pivotal role in the country's trade dynamics, could face risks from international shipping disruptions and changing maritime regulations.

To safeguard against such vulnerabilities, policies aimed at economic diversification are paramount. Promoting growth in high-tech industries, advanced manufacturing, and digital transformation can buffer the economy against the volatility inherent in a few dominant sectors. Denmark's ongoing investments in innovation, renewable energy, and technology offer a pathway toward reducing these risks by broadening the economic base.

Proactive Policy Measures: Future Directions

Denmark's economic resilience depends on its ability to adapt and respond to the evolving global landscape. The government's strategic focus on reforms in the tax system, labor market, and environmental policies is critical to addressing these external and structural risks. In the face of demographic shifts, Denmark must continue to promote policies that foster labor market participation, particularly among older workers and immigrants, and implement reforms to secure the sustainability of public pension systems.

On the international stage, Denmark must leverage its EU membership and global economic standing to ensure that its trade relationships remain robust, even as global trade dynamics shift. Pursuing further diversification of its economic sectors will reduce dependency on any single industry, while continued investments in green energy, technology, and digital innovation will position Denmark as a leader in the sustainable global economy of tomorrow.

In conclusion, while Denmark's economy remains stable and prosperous, it is imperative that the country's leadership continues to develop proactive strategies that address both the external and structural risks it faces. By implementing comprehensive reforms, fostering economic diversification, and ensuring the sustainability of its social systems, Denmark can continue to thrive in an increasingly complex and uncertain world.

Tax and Regulatory Reforms

Denmark's regulatory environment, traditionally viewed as business-friendly, is undergoing transformative reforms, especially in taxation and labor market flexibility. These changes are integral to supporting Denmark's economic goals, ensuring sustainable growth, and enhancing the nation's competitiveness in a rapidly evolving global economy. The Danish government is actively simplifying its regulatory frameworks to reduce bureaucratic hurdles and encourage private investment, while simultaneously addressing demographic and economic shifts through comprehensive policy adjustments.

Tax Reforms: Encouraging Investment and Economic Growth

Denmark's progressive tax system, while designed to support its strong welfare state, is increasingly focused on encouraging investment and enhancing the country's attractiveness as a hub for multinational enterprises. In recent years, the government has implemented strategic reforms aimed at simplifying its corporate tax structure, making it more streamlined and competitive within the European Union. These changes are expected to enhance Denmark's appeal as a location for businesses seeking favorable tax conditions, particularly in the context of rising global competition for investment.

The government's tax reforms aim to balance the need for public revenue with a desire to foster private sector growth. The lowering of corporate tax rates, for example, is part of a broader strategy to attract foreign direct investment (FDI), especially in high-tech and green industries. This aligns with

Denmark's ambition to transition to a greener economy, where investment in renewable energy and sustainability-driven sectors is critical. Furthermore, adjustments to capital gains and dividend taxes are designed to incentivize domestic and foreign investors to engage in long-term investments, particularly in innovation and green technologies.

The Denmark's fiscal policies remain focused on maintaining fiscal discipline while accommodating the rising costs associated with aging populations, climate change, and defense needs. The use of surplus government funds for long-term investment in infrastructure and green technology projects exemplifies this approach, encouraging sustainable economic growth without jeopardizing fiscal stability.

Labor Market Reforms: Fostering Flexibility and Inclusivity

In tandem with tax reform, Denmark is modernizing its labor market to address structural challenges. With a low unemployment rate and high participation among certain groups, the government is focused on enhancing labor market flexibility and increasing participation among underrepresented groups, such as older workers and immigrants. Structural changes are necessary to ensure that labor market dynamics keep pace with the evolving demands of the economy. To this end, Denmark is considering policies aimed at reducing barriers to employment for older workers, such as creating incentives for extended working lives and supporting re-skilling initiatives.

Moreover, reforms targeting immigrants and individuals with lower educational attainment are central to Denmark's strategy of improving labor market inclusivity. Given the challenges of an aging population, leveraging this untapped workforce is essential for maintaining high productivity levels. Reforms in this area include expanding vocational education programs, enhancing language skills, and providing targeted training that matches the needs of emerging sectors like technology and renewable energy.

Environmental Regulations: Driving Green Investments

Denmark has positioned itself as a global leader in green energy and environmental sustainability. The country's regulatory frameworks are increasingly aligned with its ambitious climate goals, creating a favorable environment for green investments. The government has already made significant strides in promoting renewable energy sources, with offshore wind farms, solar energy projects, and energy storage solutions at the forefront of its agenda. The government's regulatory initiatives in the environmental space are crucial to achieving the country's emissions reduction targets.

These reforms, including the simplification of permitting processes for green energy projects and the introduction of tax credits for sustainable technologies, aim to encourage both domestic and international investments in the green economy. The introduction of carbon pricing mechanisms, as well as the promotion of public-private partnerships in the renewable energy sector, will be essential in driving further innovation in clean energy technologies.

By facilitating a seamless regulatory environment for green investments, Denmark is enhancing its status as a global leader in the transition to a sustainable economy. It is of critical importance to maintain these policies to foster long-term investments in the green sector, ensuring that Denmark remains competitive on the global stage as a destination for sustainability-driven capital.

A Progressive and Flexible Regulatory Environment

In sum, Denmark's tax and regulatory reforms reflect a forward-thinking approach to economic transformation. By modernizing the tax system, enhancing labor market flexibility, and advancing environmental regulations, Denmark is preparing to meet the challenges of a changing global landscape. These reforms are not just about ensuring continued growth—they are designed to attract the investment needed to drive the country's green and digital transitions, positioning Denmark as a leading global player in sustainability and innovation. Through strategic foresight and an unwavering commitment to economic inclusivity and environmental responsibility, Denmark offers a stable and progressive regulatory environment ripe for investment.

Strategic Investment Sectors

Strategic Investment Sectors

Looking ahead, Denmark offers a range of dynamic investment opportunities that are poised to drive future economic growth. The country's strategic focus on sustainability, technological innovation, and infrastructure development has established a fertile environment for investments across several sectors. Denmark's investment landscape is undergoing a profound transformation, fueled by the country's commitments to environmental goals, advanced manufacturing, and modernization in key sectors like healthcare and biotechnology.

Infrastructure Development: Connecting Denmark to the Future

Denmark's infrastructure development is a core area of growth, bolstered by EU-backed projects and the country's long-term strategic vision. These investments in transportation, digital connectivity, and renewable energy will be essential to maintaining Denmark's global competitiveness and fostering economic sustainability. The EU-funded projects will enhance both domestic infrastructure and interconnectivity with broader European markets. Expanding transportation networks, improving energy efficiency, and investing in digital infrastructure will support Denmark's transition to a more connected and resilient economy.

The government's focus on modernizing its infrastructure aligns with its broader environmental goals, particularly the push toward renewable energy. Projects designed to strengthen the grid for offshore wind energy, improve energy storage, and facilitate the distribution of green energy are a top priority. Furthermore, there is significant potential for private investment in these areas, supported by Denmark's progressive regulatory frameworks and public-private partnership models. These projects promise not only long-term sustainability but also the creation of jobs and opportunities in construction, technology, and green industries.

Healthcare and Biotechnology: Innovation for an Aging Population

Denmark's healthcare and biotechnology sectors are gaining increasing importance, driven by the twin challenges of an aging population and advances in medical technology. The Denmark's healthcare system, renowned for its high standards, is undergoing innovation, particularly in telemedicine, eldercare, and biotechnology. These innovations are crucial to managing the demands of an older population, which requires more healthcare services, and to improving the overall quality and accessibility of care.

The strong collaboration between Denmark's public and private sectors is a key feature of this sector. Public funding combined with private innovation is driving advances in biotechnology, with opportunities for investments in areas such as personalized medicine, gene therapy, and digital health solutions. Moreover, the aging population creates additional demand for eldercare services, opening further avenues for investment in healthcare technologies and services tailored to this demographic.

As Denmark moves forward with healthcare reforms and biotechnology innovations, it is suggested that a focus on digital health solutions will be vital for improving service delivery, reducing costs, and enhancing patient outcomes. Investors looking to enter this market will find ample opportunities in the development and commercialization of health-tech solutions, which are rapidly gaining traction within Denmark's robust regulatory and research environment.

Advanced Manufacturing: Embracing Automation and Industry 4.0

The advanced manufacturing sector is another promising area for investment in Denmark. As part of its strategy to modernize industrial production, Denmark is focusing on automation and the integration of Industry 4.0 technologies. The Denmark's emphasis on high-value production, coupled with its commitment to sustainability, is driving demand for cutting-edge manufacturing solutions.

Investments in smart factories, automation, and robotics are central to Denmark's industrial modernization efforts. The government is fostering an environment conducive to the adoption of digital technologies that improve efficiency, productivity, and sustainability in manufacturing. These efforts are particularly crucial in light of Denmark's goal to remain competitive in an increasingly globalized and automated world.

Moreover, as industries move towards greater digitization, Denmark's manufacturing sector will need to adapt by embracing artificial intelligence (AI), big data analytics, and the Internet of Things (IoT). This transition to smart, data-driven manufacturing will not only position Denmark as a leader in innovation but also support the country's green transition by reducing energy consumption and waste in industrial processes.

By fostering a high-tech, green manufacturing ecosystem, Denmark provides a stable and attractive investment environment for companies looking to adopt the latest technologies while contributing to global sustainability goals.

Future-Proofing Denmark's Economy

Denmark's strategic investment sectors—spanning infrastructure, healthcare and biotechnology, and advanced manufacturing—are aligned with both global and domestic priorities. By investing in these areas, Denmark is positioning itself at the forefront of Europe's digital and green revolutions. The country's strong institutional frameworks, coupled with its progressive regulatory environment, offer investors a unique opportunity to participate in high-growth industries that drive both economic and environmental sustainability. Through these forward-looking investments, Denmark is not only addressing immediate economic challenges but also securing long-term prosperity and global competitiveness.

Denmark's ambitious transformation offers exciting opportunities for investors willing to support the country's vision of a sustainable, technologically advanced, and inclusive future.

Denmark's Path to a Sustainable Future

Denmark's journey toward a sustainable future is built on a foundation of fiscal prudence, technological innovation, and green leadership. With the right regulatory support, a clear commitment to ESG principles, and a forward-looking fiscal and tax strategy, Denmark offers a unique environment for investors seeking both stability and growth. The ongoing regulatory reforms and the transition to a greener, more technologically advanced economy signal a future ripe for innovation-driven investments.

Chapter (12)

Romania's Economic and Investment Landscape: Resilience, Reforms, and Strategic Growth

Romania, located in Southeastern Europe, has a population of approximately 19 million people and covers an area of around 238,397 square kilometres. The country's economy, which saw robust growth of 4.7% in 2022, has faced some slowdown in 2023 due to inflationary pressures and weaker external demand. Real GDP growth for FY24 is forecasted at around 2.7%, as domestic consumption, driven by rising real wages, and external demand are expected to support the recovery. Romania's nominal GDP for FY24 is projected at approximately €343 billion.

Romania stands as a beacon of adaptability and ambition in a rapidly changing economic landscape. Its story over the past few years is one of navigating global and regional disruptions, from the pandemic to geopolitical unrest, while advancing its long-term objectives of economic convergence with the European Union. The 2023 IMF report paints a detailed picture of an economy leveraging resilience, underpinned by regulatory reforms, fiscal restructuring, and a commitment to sustainable growth. This chapter unpacks Romania's economic trajectories, investment opportunities, and regulatory advancements, offering a nuanced view of its evolving landscape.

Economic Performance: Stability Amid Global Uncertainty

Romania has experienced a dual narrative in its economic performance, balancing resilience with challenges. The economy posted robust growth of 4.7% in 2022, buoyed by consumption and investment. However, the first half of 2023 revealed a slowdown to 1.9% year-on-year growth, as inflationary pressures weakened real incomes and external demand remained subdued.

Public and private investments have accelerated, supported by inflows of European Union funds under the Recovery and Resilience Facility (RRF). These funds have been pivotal in modernizing infrastructure, boosting energy security, and fostering digital transformation. As growth is projected to recover modestly to 2.75% in 2024 and stabilize around a medium-term potential of 3.75%, the economy's ability to sustain this trajectory depends on improving productivity and addressing structural inefficiencies.

Inflation and Monetary Policy: Anchoring Stability in Volatile Times

Inflation has been a defining challenge for Romania, with consumer prices peaking at 16.8% in late 2022 before gradually declining to 8.8% by September 2023. Core inflation remains stubbornly elevated, driven by strong wage growth and tight labor market conditions. The National Bank of Romania (NBR) has maintained a cautious monetary stance, raising policy rates to 7% in early 2023 to combat price pressures.

It is crucial to continue this prudence. Relaxation of monetary policy should only occur once inflation, including core components, is firmly within the NBR's target band. Additionally, the report underscores the need for greater exchange rate flexibility to improve resilience to external shocks and enhance monetary policy transmission.

The challenge extends beyond inflation management to structural issues. With a partially euroized financial system and limited credit penetration, reforms to deepen financial markets and reduce reliance on foreign exchange loans are critical. Improved data collection on inflation expectations and a more comprehensive communication strategy by the NBR will further strengthen policy effectiveness.

Fiscal Policy: A Balancing Act Between Consolidation and Growth

Romania's fiscal policy is at a crossroads, grappling with large deficits and increasing debt while pursuing vital public investments. The fiscal deficit is projected to remain elevated at 6% of GDP in 2023, well above the 4.4% target agreed with the European Commission. There is a need for substantive fiscal reforms to reduce the deficit to below 3% by 2025.

Recent fiscal packages represent important initial steps.
These include reducing VAT exemptions, broadening the
personal income tax base, and introducing turnover taxes on
certain sectors. However, these measures alone are
insufficient. The IMF advocates for additional revenue-
generating reforms, such as closing tax loopholes, further
streamlining VAT rates, and implementing a reformed
property tax system. Enhanced tax administration, supported
by digitalization and increased penalties for evasion, is also
crucial.

The report highlights that fiscal consolidation must be
carefully balanced with maintaining essential investments in
infrastructure, healthcare, and education. Romania's success
in absorbing EU funds will be instrumental in achieving this
balance. RRF allocations, amounting to 1.5% of GDP
annually through 2026, provide a unique opportunity to
address structural gaps without overburdening public
finances.

Investment Landscape: Harnessing EU Opportunities

Investment, both public and private, remains a cornerstone
of Romania's growth strategy. Leveraging EU funds to
modernize infrastructure, expand renewable energy capacity,
and foster digitalization is imperative. Romania's
performance in absorbing EU funds has improved
significantly, with milestones under the RRF being met at a
steady pace. However, further strengthening the

coordination and implementation of investment projects is necessary to maximize impact.

Private sector investment, particularly in green technologies, holds vast potential. Romania's abundant renewable energy resources, including wind and solar, position it as a leader in Europe's green energy transition. The National Hydrogen Strategy, coupled with initiatives to decarbonize transport and housing, exemplifies the country's ambition to become a hub for green value chains. Encouraging private sector participation through streamlined regulatory frameworks and enhanced public-private partnerships will be vital in sustaining this momentum.

Regulatory Reforms: Laying the Groundwork for Sustained Growth

Regulatory reforms have been central to Romania's economic strategy. Several critical advancements aimed at improving governance, strengthening fiscal discipline, and enhancing public sector efficiency:

State-Owned Enterprises (SOEs): A new independent agency is being established to monitor SOE performance, alongside legislation to strengthen board member appointment criteria. These reforms aim to increase transparency and efficiency in a sector that remains critical to Romania's economy.

Tax Policy: The introduction of a tax policy unit within the Ministry of Finance represents a step toward greater predictability and planning. This unit is expected to develop medium-term strategies, ensuring that tax changes are well-communicated and implemented.

Digital Transformation: Efforts to digitize public services, including tax administration and government cloud infrastructure, are accelerating. These initiatives aim to reduce bureaucracy, improve service delivery, and combat informality.

Anti-Corruption Measures: Strengthening anti-corruption institutions, enhancing asset recovery mechanisms, and improving conflict-of-interest regulations are priorities. These reforms will bolster investor confidence and improve Romania's overall business environment.

Climate Policy: Updates to the Integrated National Energy and Climate Plan (INECP) focus on phasing out coal, expanding renewable energy investments, and introducing stricter energy efficiency standards. Complementary measures, such as carbon taxes, are also under consideration to support decarbonization efforts.

Labor Market and Human Capital: Unlocking Romania's Potential

Romania's labor market presents both challenges and opportunities. With one of the lowest labor force participation rates in the EU, particularly among women, targeted policies are needed to unlock untapped potential. Investments in childcare infrastructure, flexible work arrangements, and education quality are essential to boosting participation and productivity.

Demographic trends, including an aging population and continued emigration, further underscore the urgency of these reforms. Addressing skill mismatches and fostering vocational training programs will help align the labor force with Romania's evolving economic needs.

Green Transition: Toward a Sustainable Economy

Romania's green transition is both a necessity and an opportunity. The country has made significant progress in reducing greenhouse gas emissions, but achieving net-zero by 2050 requires transformative investments across sectors. Romania's potential to lead in renewable energy production, particularly green hydrogen, while addressing challenges in transport and housing emissions is viable.

Policy tools, such as carbon taxes and energy efficiency incentives, will play a pivotal role in driving this transition. Ensuring these measures are socially inclusive, with targeted support for vulnerable households, will be key to their success.

Conclusion: A Nation at the Threshold of Transformation

Romania's economic and investment landscape reflects a nation poised for transformation. With a focus on fiscal discipline, regulatory reforms, and strategic investments, Romania is well-positioned to achieve its long-term goals of economic convergence and sustainable growth. As it navigates this complex terrain, the country's success will depend on its ability to harmonize short-term imperatives with long-term ambitions, ensuring a prosperous future for all.

Chapter (13)

Czech Republic: A Strategic Economic and Investment Landscape in Transition

The Czech Republic, located in Central Europe, spans an area of approximately 78,866 square kilometres. With a population of around 11 million in 2024, it is a relatively small but highly industrialized nation. The country's economy, which was hit by the pandemic and the ongoing geopolitical crisis, is showing signs of recovery. The real GDP growth for FY24 is expected to rebound to 1.2%, largely driven by domestic demand, which includes a recovery in consumption and investment. Czechia's nominal GDP is projected to reach around $326 billion.

The Czech Republic is charting a course through a complex economic environment characterized by post-pandemic adjustments, structural shifts, and heightened global uncertainties. Leveraging its strong institutional framework, EU integration, and a stable financial sector, the country offers a dynamic yet challenging landscape for investors. Insights from the IMF's 2023 Article IV consultation shed light on the Czech Republic's economic recovery trajectory, fiscal policies, and investment potential, presenting a roadmap for navigating this evolving market.

Economic Recovery Amid Structural Adjustments

After a challenging economic contraction in 2023, the Czech economy is expected to recover modestly in 2024, with GDP growth projected at 1.2%, driven by a rebound in consumption, moderated inflation, and net exports. The country's economic environment reflects both resilience and the need for adaptation to longer-term structural challenges.

Economic Dynamics

Growth Trends: The economy contracted by 0.4% in 2023, reflecting falling household consumption due to real wage erosion and uncertainty. Growth is forecast to accelerate to 2.5% in 2025, supported by recovering investment and consumption.

Inflation Pressures: Inflation, which peaked at 18% in 2022, declined to 8.5% by late 2023. Disinflation is supported by falling commodity prices, lower energy costs, and subdued domestic demand. Inflation is expected to meet the central bank's 2% target by early 2025, contingent on maintaining a tight monetary policy stance.

Labor Market Resilience: Despite the economic slowdown, the Czech unemployment rate remained exceptionally low at 2.8% in 2023. While real wages fell during the inflationary peak, they began recovering in late 2023 as nominal wage growth outpaced inflation.

Risks to Growth and Inflation

Downside risks include potential global energy price volatility, prolonged geopolitical tensions, and domestic inflationary pressures from strong wage growth. Upside risks to inflation also include potential repricing due to energy subsidies being withdrawn and higher administered prices in 2024.

Fiscal Policies: Balancing Consolidation and Transformation

The Czech Republic's fiscal strategy is focused on reducing the general government deficit while simultaneously addressing long-term spending pressures stemming from an aging population and the transition to a greener, more digitalized economy. Prudent fiscal management to ensure macroeconomic stability is crucial, especially in light of the ongoing global shifts and domestic challenges such as population aging and the decarbonization drive.

The general government deficit is targeted to decline from 3.6% of GDP in 2023 to 2.2% in 2024, a significant reduction supported by fiscal consolidation measures. While fiscal consolidation is essential to stabilize public finances, it should also be flexible enough to accommodate shocks and maintain support for economic transformation. The key fiscal measures underpinning this consolidation include:

Tax adjustments, such as a higher corporate income tax rate and increases in excise taxes on alcohol, tobacco, and gambling.

VAT restructuring, which aims to simplify the tax structure by consolidating reduced VAT rates into a single 12% rate.

Public sector expenditure reductions, notably through cuts in national subsidies and streamlining government operations, which will reduce public sector wages and eliminate subsidies not linked to specific social or economic goals.

These fiscal measures are expected to generate about 1.5% of GDP in additional fiscal gains in 2024, significantly contributing to the deficit reduction goal.

Debt and Deficit Management

Public Debt Trajectory:

Public debt is projected to remain stable at 44.2% of GDP in 2023, reflecting a prudent fiscal stance despite the challenges posed by the pandemic and global economic uncertainties. Debt is expected to gradually decline to 42.5% of GDP by 2028, maintaining a level well below the EU average. This provides the Czech government with fiscal space to address future shocks, including those from the green and digital transition, as well as any potential demographic pressures due to population aging.

Fiscal Consolidation Measures:

The fiscal consolidation program is aimed at ensuring debt sustainability over the medium term. The 2024 fiscal plan includes measures to control expenditure growth, particularly through the removal of inefficient subsidies, and increase revenues through higher taxes. Notably:

Excise tax hikes and the **corporate income tax increase** are part of the effort to bring in more revenue while ensuring that the tax burden remains sustainable and does not overly stifle economic growth.

The restructuring of the VAT system will help make the tax regime more efficient and ensure that it can better meet the demands of a transforming economy.

Streamlining public sector spending, including reductions in non-essential subsidies, will help keep public sector operations lean and focused on key priorities.

These efforts are expected to contribute to a cyclically adjusted fiscal deficit contraction of 1.3% of potential GDP, which is aligned with the Czech Republic's fiscal responsibility framework (FRA). The FRA's long-term objective is to ensure that the public debt-to-GDP ratio remains sustainable, with a structural balance target of -0.75% of GDP by 2028.

Structural Reforms

Tax System Modernization:

As part of the broader fiscal strategy, a more comprehensive overhaul of the tax system is probably the right model. This includes reintroducing pre-pandemic personal income tax rates to ensure that tax revenues grow in line with GDP. Additionally, expanding property taxes will help make the tax system more progressive and ensure that it better supports the transformation towards a green economy.

Pension Reform:

There is a clear need for further pension reform to address the long-term sustainability of the system, particularly in light of demographic changes. The recommended reforms include:

Linking the retirement age to life expectancy, which would help align pension expenditures with the demographic realities of an aging population.

Closing the pension system's actuarial deficit by implementing measures to ensure that future pension obligations remain manageable without relying too heavily on future generations to bear the financial burden.

These structural reforms are vital for ensuring the long-term fiscal sustainability of the Czech Republic, enabling the government to balance the needs of an aging population with the demands of economic transformation.

While fiscal consolidation is necessary, it must be accompanied by investment in the country's green and digital future, ensuring that the Czech Republic remains competitive and resilient in a rapidly changing global economy.

Strategic Investment Opportunities

The Czech Republic's alignment with EU priorities, particularly in sustainability and digital transformation, enhances its appeal as a hub for forward-looking investments. The country's focus on green and digital transitions, coupled with substantial EU funding and domestic incentives, opens up significant opportunities for strategic investments.

Green Transition

The Czech government is committed to decarbonization, with a strategic focus on renewable energy, energy efficiency, and carbon pricing mechanisms. Through its green transition, Czechia aims to phase out coal by 2033 and significantly increase the share of renewables in its energy mix, reaching 30% by 2030 and a further rise in nuclear power to 33% by 2040 opportunities:

Renewable Energy: There is significant potential in the development of solar, wind, and energy storage projects. These sectors will be integral in increasing the share of renewables in the energy mix and aligning with EU climate goals.

Sustainable Mobility: The Czech government is also investing heavily in low-emission vehicles, including electric and hydrogen-powered transport, which will create demand for electric vehicle infrastructure, including charging stations and cycling pathways .

Circular Eesilient Technologies: Investments in circular economy solutions, including recycling infrastructure and technologies that improve energy efficiency in both residential and public buildings, present promising opportunities. The Czech Republic's Recovery and Resilience Plan (RRP) includes €1.6 billion dedicated to energy efficiency projects.

Digital Economy

The Czech actively advancing its digital transformation to address challenges such as labor shortages and to improve productivity across sectors.

A focus on upgrading information technology infrastructure, expanding broadband networks, and fostering automation is driving this shift. Key Areas for Investment:

Artificial Intelligence (AI) and **e-health technologies** are among the top areas for investment, especially as businesses look to modernize their operations and improve service delivery in sectors like healthcare and manufacturing.

Advanced Manufacturing Automation: As ry pushes for greater digital integration, there is growing demand for robotics, AI-driven manufacturing processes, and digital twin technologies that improve operational efficiency and reduce costs in manufacturing industries.

Financial and Real Estate

The financial system remains robust, with high capital adequacy ratios and strong liquidity, positioning it well to support economic transformation despite challenges such as monetary tightening. Profitability in the banking sector has recovered, with low non-performing loans, and financial stability risks appear contained, despite increased risks from foreign currency corporate loans.

In the real estate sector, prices have stabilized after rapid growth, and the market is transitioning towards a more sustainable framework. Policy reforms are underway to improve housing supply and affordability. This includes activating vacant housing stock, reforming property taxes, and reducing incentives for short-term rentals, which are expected to have a stabilizing effect on property prices and rents.

These developments present a broad spectrum of investment opportunities in both the green and digital sectors, as well as in areas driving economic resilience, including finance and real estate. The Czech Republic is positioning itself as a key player in the European green and digital economy, making it a prime destination for strategic, future-oriented investments.

Challenges and Risks

The Czech Republic faces a series of **structural challenges** that will significantly shape its economic and investment landscape in the medium term. These challenges, ranging from demographic shifts to external geopolitical uncertainties, require a comprehensive policy response and present both risks and opportunities for strategic investments.

Aging Demographics

The aging population in the Czech Republic is one of the most pressing long-term challenges facing the economy. As the share of elderly citizens increases, the country is likely to experience labor supply constraints that could affect economic growth, productivity, and fiscal sustainability. With fewer working-age individuals, the strain on public finances will intensify due to increased demand for pensions, healthcare, and social services. These demographic trends call for urgent reforms in both workforce policies and the pension system to ensure long-term fiscal sustainability and economic stability.

Labor Market Reforms: There is a growing need to adapt the labor market to the realities of an aging population. This includes creating incentives for older workers to remain in the workforce longer, improving skills development for younger workers, and fostering more inclusive employment practices for groups such as women, people with disabilities, and immigrants.

Pension System Sustainability: The fiscal burden from pensions will likely increase as life expectancy rises. The government has already taken initial steps towards reform by proposing measures such as linking the retirement age to life expectancy. However, further reforms will be necessary to close the actuarial deficit in the pension system and ensure intergenerational fairness.

Geopolitical and Economic Uncertainties

The Czech Republic remains highly exposed to external shocks due to its position within the EU and its reliance on global trade and energy markets. The ongoing geopolitical tensions, particularly stemming from Russia's invasion of Ukraine, have already disrupted supply chains and led to significant volatility in energy prices. These disruptions, along with the risk of further regional conflicts, pose challenges for both economic stability and energy security in the medium term.

Supply Chain Vulnerabilities: As a key player in the EU's manufacturing and export sectors, the Czech economy is heavily reliant on global supply chains. Continued disruptions, whether from geopolitical tensions, natural disasters, or economic slowdowns in major trading partners, could undermine productivity and competitiveness.

Energy Price Volatility: The volatility in energy prices, especially natural gas and oil, poses risks for both businesses and households. The Czech government is already navigating a complex energy transition, aiming to reduce reliance on fossil fuels, but external price shocks could slow progress and increase fiscal pressures.

Given these vulnerabilities, the Czech financial sector should remain vigilant against potential currency depreciation, rising interest rates, or other shocks that may affect the stability of the koruna and the broader economy. It is recommended that the government maintain a prudent fiscal stance to ensure sufficient fiscal space to respond to unforeseen external challenges.

Climate Adaptation

The Czech Republic is facing a critical transition as it works to meet EU climate targets. These targets, which are designed to reduce greenhouse gas emissions and accelerate the shift to renewable energy sources, will require significant public and private investment. The country's reliance on coal, along with its heavy dependence on traditional fossil fuel-based energy sources, presents both a challenge and an opportunity.

Transition to Renewable Energy: A major focus of Czech climate policy is increasing the share of renewable energy in the national energy mix. However, this transition requires substantial investments in renewable energy infrastructure, including solar, wind, and hydropower projects. Additionally, energy storage solutions and grid modernization will be crucial to accommodate fluctuating renewable energy generation.

Carbon Pricing: The implementation of carbon pricing mechanisms, as part of EU-wide climate policies, will create both challenges and opportunities. While carbon pricing may raise energy costs in the short term, it could incentivize innovation in low-carbon technologies and support the development of green industries. The Czech Republic must balance the economic costs of this transition with the long-term benefits of sustainable growth.

As part of this broader climate adaptation effort, the Czech government is looking to boost investments in climate-resilient technologies and green infrastructure, such as energy-efficient buildings and eco-friendly transportation. However, achieving these goals will require both strong domestic policies and continued access to EU funding.

These structural challenges - aging demographics, geopolitical and economic uncertainties, and the need for climate adaptation - will shape the Czech Republic's economic trajectory and investment landscape in the medium term. Addressing these risks will require a coordinated approach that includes comprehensive social, fiscal, and environmental reforms, alongside strategic investments in green technologies, digital transformation, and labor market resilience. The Czech government has already made strides in tackling some of these challenges, but further reforms and investments are essential to ensure long-term economic sustainability and competitiveness in the global market.

Czechia's Path Forward: Resilience and Reform

The Czech Republic is at a pivotal moment in its economic transformation. The country's strategic focus on sustainability, digitalization, and fiscal discipline underpins its medium-term growth prospects. While challenges from demographic pressures and global uncertainties persist, the Czech Republic's strong institutional framework and commitment to structural reforms position it as a compelling destination for forward-looking investors seeking to navigate a rapidly evolving European landscape. Proactive risk management and alignment with ESG principles will be critical for long-term success in this dynamic market.

Chapter (14)

Finland: Navigating Challenges and Harnessing Opportunities for a Sustainable Economic Future

Finland, located in Northern Europe, is bordered by Sweden to the west, Russia to the east, and Norway to the north, with the Baltic Sea to the south. It is known for its expansive forests and numerous lakes, making up a significant part of its natural landscape. As of 2024, Finland's population is estimated to be approximately 5.5 million, with an aging demographic contributing to an increase in the old-age dependency ratio, which is projected to reach 50% by 2050s of its economy, Finland's GDP for 2024 is forecasted at approximately 286.6 billion Euros, with a modest growth rate of 0.4% following a contraction of 0.5% in 2023.

Finland stands at a crucial juncture of economic reinvention, where resilience meets ambition. Against the backdrop of global uncertainty, this Nordic nation's journey exemplifies an economy weathering structural challenges while uncovering new horizons for growth. Guided by insights from the IMF's 2024 Article IV Consultation, this chapter delves into Finland's evolving economic narrative, fiscal strategies, and vibrant investment opportunities. Finland's blend of pragmatic policymaking and forward-looking vision positions it as a hub for sustainable innovation and technological excellence.

Economic Performance: Balancing Stability and Progress

Economic Trajectory

Finland's economic landscape, while resilient, reflects a cautious recovery amid global and domestic headwinds. In 2023, the economy contracted by 0.5%, hampered by weak household incomes, declining house prices, and sluggish investment. However, a shallow recovery is forecast for 2024, with GDP projected to grow by 0.4%. By 2025, growth is expected to accelerate to 1.9%, buoyed by increased investment and labor market reforms. Finland's strategic response to these challenges highlights its potential to adapt and thrive in a rapidly changing economic environment.

Inflation Trends

The inflation narrative has shifted dramatically. After reaching 9.1% in 2022, inflationary pressures eased significantly, with average inflation projected to fall to 1.2% in 2024. Declining energy prices, moderate wage settlements, and a growing output gap have been key drivers of this disinflationary trend, restoring purchasing power for households and creating a favorable environment for consumption-led growth.

Labor Market Resilience

The Finnish labor market, a cornerstone of its economic stability, has shown remarkable strength despite rising unemployment, forecasted at 7.6% in 2024. The resilience is attributed to structural reforms and a continued focus on integrating talent and upskilling the workforce. However, challenges remain in addressing skill mismatches, particularly in high-demand sectors like technology and healthcare.

Finland's ability to navigate economic turbulence while laying the groundwork for sustainable recovery is a testament to its policy agility and robust institutional framework.

Fiscal Policy: A Delicate Balancing Act

Debt and Deficit

Finland's fiscal landscape reflects the dual pressures of managing short-term challenges and ensuring long-term sustainability. The fiscal deficit widened to 2.5% of GDP in 2023 due to increased spending on energy compensation, defense, and social services. Public debt rose to 76% of GDP, surpassing Nordic peers. Without corrective measures, debt is expected to reach 85% by 2028. The government has set an ambitious target to reduce the fiscal deficit to 1% of GDP by 2027 through a combination of spending cuts and employment-driven fiscal gains.

Strategic Adjustments

The government's fiscal strategy emphasizes efficiency and innovation. Initiatives to streamline social benefits, reduce inefficiencies in healthcare, and recalibrate the taxation framework signal a shift toward a more sustainable fiscal model. To address fiscal challenges, several tax policy adjustments could be considered by the Finnish tax authorities to enhance revenue while supporting green transformation, including:

Excise Tax Indexation: Implementing automatic adjustments to excise taxes to maintain their real value over time.

Carbon Taxation Expansion: Broadening the scope of carbon taxes to support environmental objectives and generate additional revenue.

Value-Added Tax (VAT) Standardization: Harmonizing VAT rates to simplify the tax system and improve efficiency.

Dividend Taxation Revisions: Modifying the taxation of dividends from non-listed companies to enhance fairness and revenue generation

These policies underscore Finland's commitment to fiscal responsibility, aiming to stabilize public finances while fostering economic growth.

Investment Opportunities: Innovation and Sustainability at the Core

Green Economy Transformation

Finland's pledge to achieve carbon neutrality by 2035 places it at the forefront of the global green economy. Significant progress has been made in expanding renewable energy capacity, with offshore wind and nuclear power leading the charge. Public-private partnerships and favorable regulatory frameworks are creating fertile ground for investments in green technologies, from biofuels to energy storage solutions. However, challenges such as the declining role of forests as carbon sinks call for enhanced strategies in forestry management and carbon pricing.

Digital Innovation

Known for its technological acumen, Finland offers a dynamic ecosystem for digital transformation. Investments in research and development are projected to reach 4% of GDP by 2030, with a focus on artificial intelligence, health-tech, and advanced manufacturing. Finland's vibrant startup culture and robust digital infrastructure create unparalleled opportunities for investors seeking to capitalize on emerging technologies.

Financial Stability: Guarding Against Vulnerabilities

Finland's financial system, though resilient, faces challenges that require proactive policy measures to mitigate risks and bolster stability. In response, the Finnish authorities have introduced significant reforms aimed at enhancing the robustness of the banking and financial sectors. Two key measures include the reinstatement of the systemic risk buffer (SyRB) and the introduction of a positive credit register. These reforms exemplify Finland's forward-thinking approach to addressing vulnerabilities and preparing for future uncertainties.

Reinstatement of the Systemic Risk Buffer (SyRB)

The systemic risk buffer is a macroprudential tool designed to protect the banking sector against systemic risks that could arise from broader economic or financial instability. This buffer, which had been temporarily reduced during the pandemic to support credit growth and economic recovery, has now been reinstated to its pre-pandemic level of 1% for credit institutions.

Key Implications of the SyRB Reinstatement:

Enhanced Resilience: By requiring banks to hold additional capital, the SyRB strengthens the banking sector's ability to absorb losses during periods of economic stress, thereby reducing the likelihood of a financial crisis.

Counteracting Emerging Risks: The reinstatement reflects the authorities' assessment of rising systemic risks, particularly in the real estate sector and cross-border exposures to Nordic markets. These risks have been exacerbated by high household indebtedness and declining house prices.

Proactive Risk Management: The return of the SyRB signals a shift from pandemic-era easing policies to a focus on long-term stability, ensuring that the banking system remains well-capitalized to withstand potential macroeconomic shocks.

The reinstatement also underscores Finland's commitment to adhering to European and international regulatory standards, enhancing its financial sector's credibility and resilience in a challenging global environment.

Introduction of a Positive Credit Register

The positive credit register is a centralized database that collects and stores detailed information about individual borrowers' credit obligations, including loans and repayment history. This tool represents a transformative step toward improving transparency and credit risk assessment in Finland's financial system.

Key Benefits of the Positive Credit Register:

Enhanced Risk Assessment: By providing lenders with access to accurate and comprehensive credit data, the register helps financial institutions better assess borrowers' creditworthiness, reducing the risk of over-lending or excessive household indebtedness.

Preventing Over-Indebtedness: The register is a critical tool in addressing Finland's high household debt levels, which stand at approximately 124% of net disposable income. It enables financial institutions to identify borrowers at risk of default and implement measures to prevent further financial strain.

Strengthened Macroprudential Oversight: The register provides regulators and policymakers with granular data to monitor trends in household and corporate lending. This data is invaluable for designing targeted macroprudential policies and mitigating systemic risks.

Consumer Benefits: For consumers, the register promotes fairer lending practices by ensuring that credit decisions are based on accurate and complete financial information.

The introduction of the positive credit register aligns Finland with best practices observed in other advanced economies, enhancing the efficiency and stability of its credit market.

Holistic Impact on Financial Stability

Together, the reinstatement of the systemic risk buffer and the introduction of the positive credit register represent a comprehensive strategy to fortify Finland's financial system. While the SyRB focuses on strengthening banks' capacity to withstand systemic risks, the credit register addresses vulnerabilities at the household and institutional levels by promoting responsible lending and borrowing practices.

These reforms are particularly timely given Finland's current financial challenges, including high household debt, vulnerabilities in the real estate market, and dependence on short-term wholesale funding. By implementing these measures, Finnish authorities have demonstrated a proactive approach to ensuring that the financial system remains robust and adaptable, capable of supporting sustainable economic growth in an increasingly complex global environment.

Strategic Challenges and Opportunities

Demographic Shifts and Labor Market Pressures

Finland's aging population and declining birth rate present significant challenges. The old-age dependency ratio, already among the highest in the OECD, underscores the need for policies that incentivize labor force participation and attract international talent. The government's Talent Boost initiative, aimed at addressing skill shortages through targeted immigration, represents a critical step in bolstering the workforce.

Innovation and Competitiveness

Finland's focus on research and development aligns with its vision of becoming a global leader in innovation. Strategic investments in education, coupled with initiatives to reduce skill mismatches, are essential to maintaining its competitive edge in high-value sectors such as digital technologies and clean energy.

Investment Hotspots

Renewable Energy: Offshore wind, biofuels, and nuclear energy projects align with Finland's ambitious climate goals and present lucrative opportunities for investors.

Health-Tech and Biotechnology: With an aging population driving demand for advanced healthcare solutions, Finland's health-tech sector is poised for exponential growth.

Advanced Manufacturing: Finland's automation-driven industrial strategies align with broader EU objectives, making it a hub for cutting-edge manufacturing technologies.

Finland's Journey Ahead

Finland's economic trajectory reflects a nation that combines resilience with innovation. As it navigates structural challenges and capitalizes on emerging opportunities,

Finland's commitment to sustainability and technological excellence will shape its future. For investors, Finland offers a compelling blend of stability, innovation, and green growth, making it a destination of choice for those seeking transformative opportunities in a rapidly evolving global landscape.

This chapter illuminates Finland's economic and investment potential, offering a nuanced perspective on the interplay of challenges and opportunities in one of Europe's most forward-thinking economies.

Chapter (15)

Portugal: A Story of Resilience, Reform, and Opportunity

Portugal, located in Southern Europe, covers an area of approximately 92,090 square kilometres. The country has a population of around 10.3 million people in 2024. Portugal's economy has rebounded strongly from the pandemic, with real GDP growth projected at 1.9% for FY24, driven by robust domestic consumption, net exports, and investment supported by EU funds. The nominal GDP for 2024 is forecasted at €278.1 billion, with a positive fiscal position reflecting reduced public debt.

Portugal's economic journey is a testament to resilience and forward-looking ambition. Emerging from a series of global shocks, the country has positioned itself as a dynamic player in the Euro Area (EA), combining robust fiscal discipline with innovative approaches to economic transformation. In the face of aging demographics, low productivity, and modest investment levels, Portugal is leveraging its unique assets and EU support to drive green and digital revolutions. This chapter delves into Portugal's economic performance, fiscal and regulatory strategies, investment climate, and its transformative aspirations, painting a picture of a nation poised for sustainable and inclusive growth.

Economic Performance: A Dynamic Recovery and Structural Realities

Portugal's economy has shown remarkable agility, outperforming its pre-pandemic trajectory and the EA average. The rapid rebound of 6.8% GDP growth in 2022 underscored the economy's ability to adapt, fueled by robust private consumption, booming tourism, and strategic investments under the EU's Recovery and Resilience Plan (RRP). However, growth moderated to 2.3% in 2023 as tighter global financial conditions and weaker external demand tempered the momentum.

Looking ahead, Portugal anticipates a balanced growth path of 1.9% in 2024, accelerating slightly to 2.3% in 2025. Inflation, once a formidable challenge, has decelerated from a peak of 10.6% in late 2022 to a projected average of 2.5% in 2024, reflecting effective fiscal and monetary interventions.

While the economic trajectory is commendable, medium-term growth faces headwinds from an aging population, labor market rigidities, and a persistent productivity gap. Yet, Portugal's ability to innovate and its vibrant export sectors offer bright spots in an otherwise subdued outlook.

Fiscal Policy: Strengthening Stability Amid Strategic Priorities

Portugal's fiscal achievements are among the most impressive in the EA. The country's fiscal surplus of 1.2% of GDP in 2023 and a sharp reduction in public debt to 99% of GDP (down from 135% in 2020) underscore its disciplined approach to fiscal management. This progress was bolstered by buoyant tax revenues, withdrawal of pandemic-related expenditures, and targeted cost-of-living support.

In 2024, the government plans an expansionary fiscal stance to support domestic demand while preserving long-term fiscal health. Tax reforms, including personal income tax (PIT) reductions for young workers and corporate tax incentives for innovation, aim to retain talent and stimulate investment. Over the medium term, fiscal policy will pivot towards a neutral stance, ensuring debt reduction and creating fiscal buffers.

A key challenge lies in addressing aging-related expenditure pressures, particularly in pensions and healthcare, while improving spending efficiency. The government's commitment to reducing tax expenditures, streamlining public sector compensation, and integrating performance reviews into budgetary processes will be critical in balancing fiscal prudence with growth imperatives.

Investment Climate: Unlocking Potential in Green and Digital Sectors

Portugal stands at the cusp of transformative investment opportunities, driven by its commitment to sustainability, digital innovation, and inclusive growth. The government's strategic focus on the green and digital transitions positions Portugal as a hub for forward-looking investments.

Green Economy Transition

Portugal's ambition to achieve carbon neutrality by 2045 sets the stage for expansive investments in renewable energy, energy efficiency, and sustainable infrastructure. Major initiatives include:

Renewable Energy Projects: Investments in offshore wind, solar energy, and green hydrogen are poised to redefine Portugal's energy landscape.

Carbon Pricing Mechanisms: The reactivation of carbon tax adjustments and integration into the EU's extended emissions trading system (ETS2) will incentivize green innovation while supporting fiscal revenues.

Energy-Efficient Infrastructure: Public-private partnerships will play a vital role in modernizing transportation and building systems, contributing to decarbonization.

Digital Transformation

Portugal's digital transformation strategy, underpinned by RRP funds, emphasizes enhancing connectivity, fostering innovation, and building a tech-savvy workforce. Key areas of focus include:

Smart Specialization: The National Strategy for Smart Specialization targets ICT, digital finance, and health tech as key growth areas.

Broadband Expansion: Investments in mobile broadband infrastructure aim to bridge connectivity gaps and ensure equitable digital access.

AI and R&D Investments: Prioritizing research and development (R&D) and artificial intelligence (AI) readiness will be instrumental in maintaining competitiveness.

Real Estate and Housing

Portugal's real estate market continues to attract global attention. However, surging housing prices and affordability concerns have prompted government action. Initiatives to relax construction regulations, repurpose public buildings, and incentivize large-scale housing projects reflect a commitment to balancing market demands with social equity.

Regulatory and Tax Landscape: Reform for Competitiveness and Equity

Portugal's regulatory and tax framework is undergoing a transformation to foster economic inclusivity, attract foreign investment, and enhance competitiveness. Notable developments include:

Corporate Tax Reforms: A phased reduction of corporate income tax rates, coupled with R&D tax incentives, is designed to stimulate entrepreneurship and innovation.

Targeted Personal Tax Incentives: Preferential PIT rates for young professionals and skilled foreigners aim to retain and attract talent, although concerns about equity and system complexity remain.

Property and Carbon Tax Adjustments: Proposed increases in property taxes and the resumption of carbon tax mechanisms signal a shift toward environmentally and socially responsible taxation.

Regulatory simplifications, particularly in construction and services, and the introduction of a comprehensive tax reform strategy reflect a forward-thinking approach to economic governance.

Strategic Challenges and Pathways to Transformation

Aging Population and Labor Market

Portugal's aging demographics present a structural challenge. While positive net migration offsets workforce declines, reforms to pension systems and active labor market policies will be essential in sustaining economic vitality.

Productivity Growth

Addressing Portugal's productivity gap requires a multifaceted approach. Streamlining administrative processes, reducing labor market rigidities, and fostering skills development are key to unlocking economic potential.

Infrastructure Investment

Increased public investment, particularly in transport, energy, and digital infrastructure, will enhance Portugal's competitiveness and resilience.

Conclusion: A Vision for Inclusive and Sustainable Growth

Portugal's economic outlook is shaped by its resilience, reform-minded governance, and strategic investments in transformative sectors. The country's commitment to green and digital transitions, coupled with fiscal discipline and innovative regulatory reforms, offers a compelling narrative of opportunity and growth.

As Portugal navigates its path toward sustainable development, it stands as a beacon for investors seeking to align with a future-ready economy. With the right mix of policies, Portugal has the potential to not only overcome its structural challenges but to emerge as a leader in inclusive and transformative growth.

Chapter (16)

Greece: A Strategic Economic and Investment Landscape Amid Recovery and Structural Transformation

Greece, located in Southeastern Europe, covers an area of approximately 131,957 square kilometres. The country has a population of around 10.5 million people as of 2024. Greece's economy is recovering strongly following the pandemic, with real GDP growth projected at 2.1% for FY24, driven by strong tourism, domestic demand, and continued investment fueled by Next Generation EU (NGEU) funds. The country's nominal GDP for FY24 is estimated at €233.9 billion.

Greece, having endured a decade of economic stagnation and crises, is now on a robust recovery trajectory. The economic landscape is marked by resilient growth, driven by strong tourism, bolstered investment, and continued fiscal reforms. However, substantial risks remain, particularly from inflationary pressures, public debt, demographic challenges, and climate change. This chapter delves deeper into Greece's current economic situation, the trajectory of key indicators such as GDP growth, inflation, fiscal performance, and

public debt, and the country's potential for investment across
various sectors.

Steady Economic Growth and Inflation Pressures

Greece's economy demonstrated a strong rebound from the
pandemic, with real GDP growing by 5.6% in 2022 and
projected at 2.3% in 2023. This recovery has been notably
robust, as the country's economic output surpassed pre-
pandemic levels for the first time in over a decade. For 2024,
GDP growth is projected to moderate slightly to 2.1%,
reflecting cooling momentum but still positioning Greece as
one of the stronger performers in the Eurozone.

Key drivers of this growth have included:

Tourism: A major contributor to the Greek economy,
tourism demand has significantly recovered post-pandemic,
exceeding 2019 levels. This sector alone remains a
cornerstone of Greece's economic recovery.

Investment: Boosted by Next Generation EU (NGEU)
funds, foreign direct investment (FDI), and structural
reforms, Greece has experienced a surge in investment,
particularly in sectors aligned with green and digital
transitions.

However, inflation remains a challenge, with headline
inflation decelerating from a high of 9.3% in 2022 to 4.2% in
2023, and the IMF projects a further decline to 2.8% by 2024.
Despite this, core inflation (excluding volatile food and
energy prices) remains sticky, hovering at 4.8% as of late

2023, primarily due to rising services costs and wage pressures. It is suggested that while energy prices will continue to normalize, wage increases in both the public and private sectors will exert upward pressure on inflation, complicating the ECB's inflation-targeting efforts.

Public Debt and Fiscal Sustainability

One of Greece's key achievements in recent years has been the gradual reduction of its public debt-to-GDP ratio. Following the pandemic, Greece's public debt peaked at 179.5% of GDP in 2022, but the strong post-pandemic recovery, high inflation, and fiscal consolidation efforts helped bring it down to 167.4% by 2023. The IMF forecasts a further decline to 158% by 2024.

This improvement in Greece's debt metrics is primarily due to the following factors:

Debt Structure: Greece's public debt is characterized by a favourable structure, with a large share held by official creditors, long maturities, and low fixed interest rates. This structure has shielded the country from the full effects of rising interest rates in the Eurozone.

Fiscal Consolidation: The government has implemented a growth-friendly fiscal consolidation, achieving a primary surplus (the fiscal balance excluding debt interest payments) of 1.1% of GDP in 2023, up from 0.1% in 2022. It is projected that Greece will maintain a primary surplus of 2.1% of GDP in 2024, underscoring the country's fiscal discipline.

However, challenges remain:

Structural Imbalances: Despite fiscal progress, Greece still faces structural imbalances, including low household savings and inadequate levels of investment, which weigh on medium-term growth prospects. It is noteworthy to mention the risks posed by demographic trends, particularly the decline in the working-age population, which is expected to decrease by 1% annually until 2030.

Fiscal Risks: While Greece's debt structure has helped reduce refinancing risks, higher public spending demands—especially on pensions and healthcare—could pressure future fiscal space, necessitating continued reforms.

External Sector Dynamics and Current Account Deficits

The current account of Greece has been a focal point for economic evaluation due to its persistent deficits. In 2022, the current account deficit reached 10.7% of GDP, primarily driven by elevated import costs stemming from high global energy prices and the robust domestic demand fueled by post-pandemic economic recovery. However, as global energy prices began to decline and Greece experienced a surge in tourism, the external sector started showing signs of recovery. By mid-2023, the current account deficit narrowed to 7.1% of GDP, marking a notable improvement. Projections from the IMF indicate a continued decline in the deficit, estimated to reach 6.4% of GDP by the end of 2024.

Foreign Direct Investment (FDI): Foreign Direct Investment (FDI) inflows into Greece, though relatively stable, remain modest compared to the Eurozone average, highlighting ongoing challenges in fully capitalizing on its economic potential. In absolute terms, FDI reached approximately €4.9 billion in 2022, marking a significant rebound driven by improvements in investor confidence and recovery momentum post-pandemic. However, inflows slightly tapered to an estimated €4.7 billion in 2023, underscoring the need for sustained efforts to enhance the business environment. The FDI-to-GDP ratio, at -2.1% in 2023, reflects these dynamics, with projections for 2024 anticipating a further dip to -2.9% as macroeconomic headwinds and structural inefficiencies persist.

While Greece has benefited from robust investment in specific sectors like tourism, energy, and shipping, broader diversification and increased scale remain critical. Structural impediments, such as regulatory complexity, the cost of doing business, and infrastructure gaps, continue to pose challenges to unlocking Greece's full FDI potential. Nevertheless, the government's focus on targeted reforms—such as the digitization of public services, streamlining of licensing processes, and promotion of strategic investments—provides a framework for improvement.

The implementation of Greece's National Recovery and Resilience Plan (NRRP), supported by EU funds, has the potential to attract greater FDI by prioritizing key areas such as renewable energy, technology, and infrastructure development. These investments align with Greece's long-term objectives of fostering sustainable and inclusive growth. Moreover, measures to enhance competitiveness and transparency, including tax incentives for green investments and fostering partnerships with international stakeholders, are expected to play a pivotal role in expanding FDI inflows.

Sustained efforts to address structural barriers and improve
market conditions will be crucial in aligning Greece with its
Eurozone peers in FDI performance, ultimately supporting
its broader economic recovery and resilience strategy.

External Debt: Greece's external debt remains significantly
high, at 259% of GDP in 2023. While this level is substantial,
the debt profile benefits from favorable financing terms,
such as long maturities and low interest rates on official
sector loans. These conditions mitigate immediate
refinancing risks. However, the external position remains
weaker than optimal when compared to medium-term
economic fundamentals. The reduction in the current
account deficit, along with sustained economic growth and
increased investment, is expected to gradually bolster
Greece's external balance. Key Influences on External
Dynamics:

Tourism and Services: The tourism sector has been a
significant driver of recovery in the external account. As
international travel resumes, Greece has witnessed record
levels of tourist arrivals and spending, boosting service
exports and narrowing trade imbalances.

Energy Imports: The decline in global energy prices has
eased import costs, which had been a major contributor to
the current account deficit in prior years.

Export Competitiveness: While Greece's export base is
growing, it remains relatively concentrated in specific sectors
like tourism and shipping. Diversifying exports will be crucial
for achieving a more resilient external balance.

The ongoing economic reforms and targeted investment under programs such as the National Recovery and Resilience Plan (NRRP) are anticipated to strengthen the external sector further. Improved digital infrastructure, reduced regulatory barriers, and incentives for green investments could catalyse a broader and more sustainable export-driven growth model.

Labor Market and Productivity Growth

The Greek labor market has shown notable improvements. The **unemployment rate** has dropped from 12.4% in 2022 to 10.6% in 2023 and is expected to decline further to 9.2% in 2024. This marks a significant improvement over the past decade, though youth unemployment remains stubbornly high at 23.7%. Key trends in Greece's labor market include:

Real Wage Growth: **Real wages** have increased in 2023, supported by strong employment growth and a tightening labor market. The unit labor cost remains competitive within the Eurozone, contributing to Greece's improved international competitiveness.

Productivity Challenges: Although Greece has seen a recovery in labor productivity, it still lags behind the Eurozone average, particularly in sectors reliant on digital technologies and innovation. Further investment in skills development and digitalization will be critical to raising productivity levels and addressing labor shortages.

Financial System Resilience and Risks

Greece's financial system has displayed significant resilience, largely due to its strengthened banking sector. The Non-Performing Loan (NPL) ratio in the banking system fell below 5% in 2023, marking a notable improvement since the sovereign debt crisis. The banks have benefitted from policy support, including the government-backed Hercules program, which has helped address NPLs.

However, the banking sector faces ongoing challenges:

Interest Rate Risks: As interest rates in the Eurozone remain elevated, Greece's banks face potential pressure on their profitability and capital adequacy. Measures such as strengthening liquidity management and implementing macroprudential policies, including activating a counter-cyclical capital buffer to safeguard against potential systemic shocks are recommended.

Real Estate Market: The real estate market has experienced a sharp recovery, with residential property prices increasing by more than 50% since the 2017 low. However, the IMF warns that house prices are overvalued by 6-29%, depending on the methodology used, indicating the risk of a market correction if financial conditions tighten further.

Structural Reforms: Green and Digital Transitions

The Greece's medium-term growth will depend on its ability to address structural impediments and implement transformative reforms, particularly in green and digital sectors.

Green Transition: Greece has set ambitious climate goals, aiming to reduce its greenhouse gas emissions by 55% by 2030. The government has made progress in expanding renewable energy sources, but fossil fuels still dominate the energy mix, accounting for about 80% of energy consumption. Significant investments are needed to develop renewable energy infrastructure, improve energy efficiency, and modernize the electricity grid.

Digitalization: Greece has made strides in digital transformation, including the digitalization of government services, which has enhanced business productivity and tax compliance. However, the country lags behind in integrating digital technologies across sectors, especially among small and medium-sized enterprises (SMEs). Further efforts to improve digital skills, streamline regulations, and enhance the digital infrastructure will be key to raising Greece's productivity and competitiveness.

Key Takeaways for Investors

Investment in Green and Digital Sectors: Greece's strategic investment in renewable energy, digital infrastructure, and sustainable technologies offers significant growth potential. The ongoing reforms and the availability of EU funding make it an attractive destination for long-term investments in green and tech-driven sectors.

Fiscal and Debt Stability: Greece's debt trajectory is improving, but investors should monitor fiscal sustainability closely, particularly in light of the country's high public debt and ongoing structural imbalances. Fiscal reforms aimed at addressing tax evasion and increasing public investment will be critical in ensuring long-term fiscal stability.

Real Estate Caution: While the real estate market has shown strong recovery, overvaluation risks remain. Investors should approach the sector cautiously, especially given the potential for a market correction if interest rates continue to rise.

Labor Market and Productivity: With a growing labor force and improving real wage growth, Greece offers opportunities in sectors requiring skilled labor. However, addressing skill mismatches and increasing productivity through digitalization will be key to maintaining long-term competitiveness.

Conclusion: Greece's Path Forward

Greece stands at a pivotal moment in its economic journey, transitioning from a decade of crises to a phase of recovery and transformation. The country's robust GDP growth, driven by thriving tourism, targeted investments, and fiscal reforms, underscores its resilience and potential. However, the challenges ahead are equally significant, encompassing inflationary pressures, high public debt, external imbalances, and demographic constraints. These issues necessitate sustained and strategic policy interventions.

Key reforms aimed at enhancing digital and green transitions, improving labor market dynamics, and fortifying the financial system are essential for addressing structural impediments and unlocking the country's economic potential.

For investors, Greece presents a compelling mix of opportunities and risks.

Greece's strategic investments under the National Recovery and Resilience Plan (NRRP) and ongoing efforts to improve its business environment position the country as an emerging investment hub in Europe. By addressing structural weaknesses and leveraging its strengths in tourism, shipping, and energy, Greece can achieve sustained growth and bolster its role in the global economy. The journey ahead requires balancing ambition with pragmatism, ensuring that progress today translates into long-term resilience and prosperity.

Chapter (17)

Hungary: Navigating Challenges and Harnessing Opportunities for a Sustainable Economic Future

Hungary, located in Central Europe, spans an area of approximately 93,028 square kilometres. The country has a population of around 9.6 million in 2024. Hungary's economy is projected to grow by 2.3% in FY24 following a contraction of 0.9% in 2023. The country's nominal GDP for 2024 is forecasted to reach approximately $223 billion.

Hungary stands at a pivotal juncture as it emerges from a period of profound economic disruption, shaped by global crises and domestic fiscal challenges. The path forward is one of cautious optimism, where strategic reforms and sustainable growth initiatives can reshape the nation's economic trajectory. Leveraging insights from the IMF's 2024 Article IV Consultation, this chapter delves deeply into Hungary's evolving economic dynamics, fiscal landscape, and investment ecosystem, offering a nuanced perspective on its prospects.

Economic Performance: Recovery Amid Complex Challenges

Economic Trajectory

Hungary's economy is on a recovery path, with GDP growth forecasted at 2.3% in 2024 after a 0.9% contraction in 2023. This rebound, primarily driven by improved private consumption and a positive contribution from net exports, reflects a slow but steady revival. By 2025, GDP growth is expected to accelerate to 3.3% as private investment strengthens and EU funds, critical for infrastructural and digital advancement, are unlocked.

However, risks to growth remain. Persistent policy uncertainty, fiscal imbalances, and weak investor confidence could dampen the recovery. Structural inefficiencies, including the significant presence of state-owned enterprises (SOEs) in critical sectors, continue to weigh on productivity.

Inflation Trends

Inflation, once Hungary's most pressing macroeconomic challenge, has moderated significantly from a peak of 25% in early 2023 to 3.7% by mid-2024. The Magyar Nemzeti Bank's (MNB) aggressive monetary tightening, complemented by falling global commodity prices and a stronger forint, played a pivotal role in this disinflationary trajectory. However, inflationary pressures are expected to re-emerge mildly in late 2024, reaching 4.2%, before stabilizing around the MNB's 3% target by 2026.

Labor Market Dynamics

Hungary's labor market demonstrates resilience amidst economic adjustments. The unemployment rate is forecasted to rise slightly to 4.4% in 2024, reflecting a modest loosening in the market. Labor hoarding and increased workforce participation due to living cost pressures have kept employment levels relatively robust. However, challenges such as regional disparities and skill mismatches, particularly in high-demand sectors like digital technologies, remain barriers to optimizing labor productivity.

Fiscal Policy: A Balancing Act Between Stability and Reform

Debt and Deficit Dynamics

Hungary's fiscal challenges are pronounced, with the deficit at 6.7% of GDP in 2023, well above the Maastricht threshold of 3%. The IMF projects the deficit will narrow to 5% in 2024, yet remain elevated in the absence of substantial policy adjustments. Public debt, though marginally reduced to 73.5% of GDP in 2023, persists at levels significantly above pre-pandemic norms.

Gross financing needs (GFNs) are expected to remain in double digits through 2029, reflecting heightened borrowing requirements. Without corrective measures, fiscal vulnerabilities may further erode investor confidence.

Tax Rates and Reform Proposals

Hungary's tax structure is a critical lever for fiscal consolidation. Current policies rely heavily on distortive instruments such as windfall taxes and financial transaction taxes. The VAT rate, among the highest globally at 27%, generates significant revenue but is criticized for its broad application and inefficiencies. Corporate income tax (CIT) is comparatively low at 9%, contributing to Hungary's appeal as an investment destination but also limiting revenue potential.

Several tax reforms to enhance efficiency and equity are recommended:

Personal Income Tax (PIT): Introduce a higher marginal rate for high earners to complement the existing flat rate of 15%.

Corporate Taxation: Rationalize tax incentives and increase the CIT rate to align with international standards, while reducing reliance on windfall taxes.

Property Taxes: Expand and reform property taxation to generate stable, long-term revenue.

VAT Simplification: Retain the high standard VAT rate but reduce exemptions to simplify administration and increase compliance.

Expenditure Adjustments

Rationalizing subsidies, particularly energy-related ones, which accounted for 2.7% of GDP in 2023 is essential. A shift toward targeted cash transfers for vulnerable households could save approximately 0.8% of GDP by 2029. Similarly, reforms in public sector wages and goods spending, alongside prudent cuts to unproductive investments, are essential to creating fiscal space for growth-friendly initiatives.

Investment Landscape: Unlocking Potential Amidst Constraints

Green Economy Opportunities

Hungary's green transition offers compelling investment prospects. With a burgeoning battery and electric vehicle (EV) manufacturing sector, Hungary is positioning itself as a regional leader in clean energy exports. The transition, however, faces obstacles such as reliance on fossil fuel subsidies and lagging renewable energy capacity. Strategic investments in energy-efficient infrastructure, electric grids, and green technologies are imperative.

Digital Transformation

Hungary's National Digitalization Strategy highlights significant potential for innovation-driven growth. Investments in artificial intelligence (AI), advanced manufacturing, and digital infrastructure are poised to redefine Hungary's economic landscape. Nevertheless, closing regional digital divides and reskilling the workforce are critical to fully harnessing these opportunities.

Financial Sector Resilience

The banking sector, characterized by high capital adequacy ratios and profitability, has weathered recent monetary tightening. However, vulnerabilities persist, particularly in the real estate sector. Commercial real estate faces declining valuations and elevated vacancy rates, while residential markets, buoyed by government-subsidized loans, risk overheating. Phasing out interest rate caps and aligning credit allocation with market dynamics will be crucial for long-term financial stability.

Strategic Challenges and Opportunities

Structural Reforms

Hungary's productivity lags behind regional peers, largely due to systemic inefficiencies and governance shortcomings. Key reforms include:

Reducing SOE Dominance: Enhancing private sector participation and competition in critical industries.

Improving Governance: Addressing corruption and regulatory inefficiencies to unlock withheld EU funds and attract foreign investment.

Advancing Education and Skills: Targeted investments in STEM education and vocational training are critical to bridging skill gaps in emerging industries.

EU Integration

Hungary's access to €19 billion in EU funds remains contingent on judicial reforms and governance improvements. Timely resolution of these issues is vital for financing the green and digital transitions, as well as regional infrastructure development.

Regional Focus

Addressing regional inequalities through targeted incentives and infrastructure investments is critical. Disadvantaged regions present untapped opportunities for development, particularly in manufacturing and logistics.

Hungary's Journey Ahead

Hungary's economic landscape is defined by a delicate interplay of recovery, reform, and resilience. The nation's ability to balance fiscal consolidation with strategic investments in sustainability and innovation will determine its trajectory. For investors, Hungary offers a blend of transformative opportunities in green energy, digital technologies, and advanced manufacturing. However, navigating its complex regulatory and fiscal environment requires a nuanced approach. This chapter underscores the imperative for Hungary to embrace holistic reforms, fostering a resilient, inclusive, and sustainable economic future.

Chapter (18)

Slovakia: Navigating Fiscal Pressures and Green Growth Opportunities

Slovakia, located in Central Europe, covers an area of approximately 49,035 square kilometres. The country's population is around 5.5 million people in 2024. Slovakia's economy is expected to grow by 2.1% in 2024, following a slower expansion of 1.1% in 2023. The nominal GDP is projected to reach approximately €130.6 billion for FY24.

Slovakia's economic narrative in 2023 is one of careful navigation through a maze of fiscal pressures, demographic challenges, and a changing geopolitical landscape. The economy, bolstered by strong fiscal stimulus and public investment, has shown resilience amid rising commodity prices, the lingering effects of the pandemic, and supply chain disruptions. However, the journey ahead demands deep fiscal reforms and strategic shifts towards green and digital investments to unlock sustainable growth. Slovakia's long-term growth trajectory hinges on its ability to balance fiscal consolidation with the promise of green transition, infrastructure modernization, and digital transformation.

This chapter explores Slovakia's economic performance, fiscal health, labor market dynamics, and evolving investment climate. By leveraging EU funds and driving structural reforms, Slovakia is positioning itself to emerge as a leader in green energy, sustainable infrastructure, and digital innovation in Central and Eastern Europe. Yet, this transformation requires navigating the complex challenges posed by aging demographics and the need for enhanced fiscal discipline.

Economic Performance: Stabilizing Amidst Uncertainty

Economic trajectory

Slovakia's economic performance in 2023 reflects a challenging balancing act between fiscal stimulus and subdued growth. The nation's GDP growth moderated to just **1.1%** in 2023, a significant slowdown from the **1.8%** growth recorded in 2022. This decline stems from the fading effects of pandemic-era savings and negative real wage growth, which reduced consumer spending. In particular, **food and energy price inflation** put pressure on household budgets and corporate bottom lines. Yet, government spending surged with **EU-funded public investments**, helping to offset weak domestic demand.

While public sector and service industries showed significant recovery, manufacturing has struggled to regain momentum, reflecting the global slowdowns and persistent supply chain bottlenecks. On a positive note, **exports** rebounded slightly as supply conditions improved, helping to stabilize Slovakia's external balance. However, despite these adjustments, **external demand** remained sluggish throughout the year, a sentiment reflected in the broader EU economic climate.

Inflation trajectory

Slovakia's inflation trajectory has moderated since its **2022 peak** of **12.1%**. By **2023**, inflation had declined slightly to **11%** on average, but it remains one of the highest in the **Eurozone**. The decline in inflationary pressures was largely driven by a drop in **food prices**, while **core inflation**, which excludes volatile energy and food prices, stayed elevated at **11.4%**. The impact of these high inflation rates has been felt most keenly by Slovakia's **low-income households**, who bear the brunt of rising essential costs.

Employment market

In the labor market, Slovakia has made progress with **employment** stabilizing since mid-2022. The influx of foreign workers, including a significant number from **Ukraine**, has helped mitigate the decline in the working-age population. However, this has not been enough to offset the **declining working-age population**, and **hours worked per worker** remain below pre-pandemic levels by about **5%**. **Youth unemployment** remains a significant concern, with rates far exceeding the average across the **Eurozone**. Despite these challenges, the country has seen **nominal wage growth** of **8.5%** in 2023, although **real wages** lagged behind due to the inflationary pressures, leaving Slovak families with reduced purchasing power.

Fiscal Policy: A Balancing Act Between Stimulus and Consolidation

Slovakia's fiscal policy in 2023 leaned heavily on **expansionary measures**, with a fiscal deficit projected at **6.5% of GDP**, up from **2.0%** in 2022. This widening deficit reflects a combination of **higher public spending**, including energy price support for households and businesses, and an **increase in social benefits** like pensions and family allowances. These measures, while essential in cushioning the impact of high inflation and energy prices, have strained public finances, adding pressure to Slovakia's **debt trajectory**.

Despite the large fiscal expansion in 2023, Slovakia's debt level is projected to remain relatively stable at 58% of GDP. This stability owes much to negative real interest rates, which have somewhat alleviated the fiscal burden. However, this stabilization masks an underlying structural weakness, as the fiscal deficit is expected to persist at elevated levels without aggressive fiscal reforms. Slovakia's public finances face a long-term challenge due to aging demographics, which will increase pension and healthcare costs over the coming decades, putting additional strain on the budget.

In response, Slovakia's 2024 budget aims to reduce the fiscal deficit by 0.5% of GDP through a combination of tax increases (including a new bank levy, healthcare contribution hikes, and a minimum tax for corporations) and spending cuts. However, despite these measures, Slovakia faces an uphill battle to meet its fiscal consolidation targets, with the structural deficit projected to widen slightly in the short term. Looking forward, Slovakia has committed to reducing its headline deficit by 1% per year in 2025 and 2026, although this will require further adjustments and reforms.

The need for deeper fiscal reforms is evident. The government's debt brake law, which imposes a 55% debt-to-GDP cap, is slated to come into effect in 2026. While the government has suspended this cap temporarily, structural reforms are urgently needed to avoid a procyclical fiscal adjustment during economic downturns. To this end, Slovakia must ensure that any revenue windfalls or lower-than-expected expenditures are saved to help meet long-term fiscal sustainability goals.

Investment Climate: Green Transition and Digitalization at the Forefront

Slovakia's investment environment is shaped by its ambition to lead the green energy transition and spearhead digital innovation across Central and Eastern Europe. These sectors offer significant opportunities for investors, particularly as Slovakia taps into EU funds aimed at driving environmental and technological advancement. However, Slovakia's economic future will depend on its ability to harness these opportunities while addressing the risks associated with geopolitical instability, demographic changes, and fiscal sustainability.

Green Energy and Climate Investments

Slovakia's shift toward renewable energy and energy efficiency is critical to its green transition goals. The country has made notable progress in reducing its reliance on Russian energy sources, with LNG contracts and increased gas storage capacity ensuring greater energy security. The Mochovce nuclear plant, which has added substantial capacity, plays a central role in ensuring Slovakia's self-sufficiency in electricity. As the nation aligns itself with the EU's Green Deal, opportunities abound in sectors such as wind, solar, and hydrogen energy.

However, challenges remain, particularly in the transportation and building sectors, where emissions have not yet sufficiently decreased to meet EU decarbonization targets. This presents an opportunity for investors focused on clean tech, green mobility, and energy-efficient building solutions.

Digital Economy and Infrastructure

Slovakia is also positioning itself as a key player in the digital economy. With significant EU-backed investments under the Recovery and Resilience Plan (RRP), Slovakia is working to enhance its digital infrastructure, expand broadband access, and promote AI and R&D. The government is also focusing on digitizing public services, offering investors opportunities in digital infrastructure, e-government, and data-driven technologies.

However, Slovakia must overcome several barriers to realizing its digital ambitions, particularly the digital divide between urban and rural areas and the shortage of tech talent. To succeed, Slovakia will need continued investment in education, upskilling, and labor market reforms that align with the needs of the digital economy.

Real Estate and Urban Development

The Slovak real estate market has cooled in recent years, with housing prices falling by 10% in 2023 due to rising mortgage rates and falling real wages. Despite these challenges, the sector remains attractive for long-term investors, especially those focused on sustainable urban development and infrastructure projects. Slovakia's cities are in need of modernization, and projects that integrate green building practices, affordable housing, and public transport solutions align with both the EU's green goals and Slovakia's own development agenda.

Regulatory and Structural Reforms: Strengthening Sustainability

Slovakia is undergoing a significant transformation in its regulatory framework, with reforms aimed at enhancing fiscal discipline, improving public sector efficiency, and fostering a more inclusive labor market. To this end, the government has initiated a reform of the fiscal framework, strengthening its expenditure ceilings and refining the **debt brake** mechanism to ensure long-term sustainability.

In the labor market, gender equality and elderly workforce participation are areas of focus, with policies designed to increase labor force participation and address regional inequalities. By fostering social inclusion and tackling demographic challenges, Slovakia aims to boost productivity and expand its labor pool.

The financial sector remains resilient, but risks are emerging, particularly in the commercial real estate market and household debt levels. As the country navigates fiscal consolidation, the banking sector will be essential in providing the necessary liquidity and credit to support green investments and digital infrastructure projects.

Conclusion: Forging a Future-Ready Slovakia

Slovakia stands at a crossroads, balancing the need for fiscal consolidation with its ambitions for a green and digital future. The nation's focus on renewable energy, digital innovation, and inclusive growth offers substantial opportunities for both domestic and international investors. However, fiscal reforms, structural adjustments, and improved absorption of EU funds will be essential to securing Slovakia's long-term economic stability.

As Slovakia works to enhance its sustainability, competitiveness, and fiscal health, it holds the potential to emerge as a key player in the EU's green transformation. With a stable investment climate, the right mix of policy reforms, and continued commitment to its EU integration, Slovakia is poised to thrive in the coming decades, offering rich opportunities for those ready to invest in its green, digital, and socially inclusive future.

Bahaa G. Arnouk

Chapter (19)

Bulgaria: Resilience, Challenges, and Opportunities in a Transforming Economy

Bulgaria, located in Southeastern Europe, has a land area of approximately 110,994 square kilometres. In 2024, its population is projected to be around 6.5 million people. The country's economy, which is primarily service-oriented, has faced several challenges, including an aging population and a decline in the labor force. Despite these issues, Bulgaria's GDP is expected to grow by 2.7% in 2024, supported by public investment, particularly from the European Union's funds. However, the country continues to grapple with low productivity growth and a relatively high level of poverty, especially among the elderly. In 2024, the country's GDP is projected at approximately €77.5 billion.

Bulgaria's economic landscape showcases remarkable resilience despite global and domestic challenges, as highlighted in the 2024 IMF Article IV Consultation report. This chapter delves into the country's economic dynamics, fiscal challenges, employment trends, inflation trajectory, and investment potential, offering a comprehensive analysis of opportunities and areas needing reform.

Economic Overview: Resilience Through Shocks

Bulgaria's economy, though tested by political uncertainties and global shocks, demonstrates steady recovery. GDP growth slowed to 1.8% in 2023 due to a decline in private investment and inventory adjustments but is forecasted to rebound to 2.7% in 2024. Key economic metrics:

Growth Prospects: Medium-term growth is expected to stabilize at 2.5%, constrained by low productivity and demographic decline.

Inflation: Falling from 13% in 2022 to 3.2% in 2024, disinflation is driven by global energy and food price stabilization. However, core inflation remains sticky, reflecting sustained wage and pension growth.

Labor Market: With unemployment at 4.3% in 2023, the labor market remains tight but faces challenges from a shrinking workforce and skill mismatches.

Fiscal Landscape: Navigating Constraints for Growth

Bulgaria's fiscal health is marked by its low public debt, which stands among the lowest in the EU at 23.4% of GDP in 2024. While this provides some fiscal space, the country faces significant fiscal pressures. These are driven by rising social spending, particularly pension outlays, which are becoming increasingly unsustainable without adequate revenue generation. Inefficient public investment further compounds these challenges, signaling an urgent need for structural reforms to ensure long-term fiscal sustainability and inclusive growth.

Fiscal Highlights:

Deficit Trends: The fiscal deficit widened to 3.1% of GDP in 2023, a significant increase from previous years. This is largely due to increased expenditure on pensions, wages, and public investment, much of which was supported by EU funds. Revenue collection, however, fell short, declining by 2.2% of GDP in 2023, with weaker VAT returns, nontax revenues, and grants. Deficits are expected to remain elevated at similar levels through 2026 unless substantial fiscal adjustments are made. Given the pressure from aging demographics and pension needs, addressing the deficit without compromising public services will be challenging.

Debt Sustainability: Public debt remains manageable in the short term, but its upward trajectory raises concerns over the medium and long term. Debt is projected to rise to 27.0% of GDP by 2026. This modest increase is primarily driven by persistent deficits, but Bulgaria's debt levels will still be below the EU's 60% of GDP limit. Maintaining this trajectory will require a balanced approach to fiscal consolidation, focusing on boosting revenues and improving the efficiency of public investments. However, increasing debt without clear high-return investments could weaken investor confidence.

Tax Reforms: Bulgaria's tax-to-GDP ratio remains one of the lowest in the EU, underscoring the need for comprehensive tax reforms. Among the necessary measures, a move towards progressive income taxation, the elimination of VAT exemptions, and improved tax compliance are critical. It is suggested that raising corporate tax rates for large multinationals could also help increase state revenues. However, these changes must be implemented carefully to avoid exacerbating informality in the economy and to enhance overall tax collection.

Policy Imperatives:

Revenue-Enhancing Reforms: Broadening the tax base and raising corporate tax rates, particularly on multinationals, should be prioritized. This would increase revenue while also addressing income inequality. A well-structured tax compliance system, along with stronger auditing and enforcement, is essential to reduce the widespread informality that hinders tax collection. Moreover, Bulgaria should continue to pursue improvements in revenue administration, including the merging of tax agencies, which has the potential to streamline operations but requires careful management to avoid operational setbacks.

Public Investment Efficiency: Bulgaria must focus on improving the efficiency of public investment, especially in infrastructure and education. This will not only create more immediate economic benefits but also contribute to long-term growth. Reforms should ensure that these investments are aligned with development goals and that resources are allocated effectively. This requires improving governance, increasing fiscal transparency, and bolstering the capacity to absorb EU funds.

Reform State-Owned Enterprises (SOEs): The SOEs are a significant source of fiscal risk. Many of these enterprises operate inefficiently, consuming substantial fiscal resources without contributing adequately to productivity. Reforms to streamline these entities and ensure they operate effectively within a competitive market framework will help reduce fiscal pressure and improve economic outcomes.

Employment and Demographics: Overcoming Structural Barriers

Bulgaria faces a critical demographic challenge, with a shrinking and aging population that poses significant risks to long-term economic growth. The working-age population has been declining by an average of 1.5% annually over the past decade, contributing to labor shortages and constraining potential growth. As Bulgaria's population continues to age, the country faces heightened pressures on its labor market, with labor force participation declining even as demand for workers rises. This trend, combined with a high dependency ratio, amplifies the need for targeted policy interventions to sustain and enhance workforce participation. Key Initiatives are:

Education and Skills: One of the most critical areas for addressing labor market imbalances is reforming the education system and improving the skills of the workforce. Improving the efficiency of public spending on education could significantly boost educational outcomes, potentially raising PISA (Programme for International Student Assessment) scores by up to 11%. This would contribute to reducing the skills mismatch that currently hampers productivity growth. Reforming curricula to meet the demands of a modern labor market, including the integration of digital and technical skills, is essential for increasing workforce readiness. Expanding lifelong learning programs, particularly in the fields of digital technologies and artificial intelligence (AI), will help bridge Bulgaria's growing digital skills gap and improve the country's competitiveness in the global market .

Labor Market Integration: Policies targeting youth unemployment, as well as the inclusion of underrepresented groups, are key to expanding Bulgaria's labor force. High levels of youth unemployment, combined with a significant proportion of young people not in education, employment, or training (NEET), represent untapped potential. Labor market policies aimed at integrating these young individuals into the workforce—through targeted vocational training, apprenticeships, and access to education—could have a significant impact. Additionally, improving access to transportation, healthcare, and other essential services, particularly for disadvantaged groups, will help foster greater labor force participation and reduce regional disparities .

Demographic Strategies: As Bulgaria faces population decline, demographic strategies to incentivize workforce participation are vital. Policies aimed at improving conditions for working parents, such as better access to affordable childcare and more flexible work arrangements, are essential for increasing female labor force participation. Furthermore, tax incentives and social policies to encourage higher birth rates could help mitigate the adverse effects of demographic decline. Given the high levels of poverty among pensioners, reforms to the pension system, including the introduction of more sustainable financing mechanisms, are also necessary to address the long-term impact of an aging population.

In conclusion, Bulgaria's ability to overcome its demographic challenges and sustain long-term growth will depend on comprehensive structural reforms in education, labor market integration, and demographic policies. Strengthening human capital, fostering inclusivity, and improving the overall labor market environment will be critical for enhancing Bulgaria's growth potential and ensuring that its workforce is equipped for the future.

Inflation and Monetary Stability: Progress with Challenges

Inflation remains a persistent challenge for Bulgaria, although it has moderated significantly from its 2022 peak of 13% to a projected 3.2% in 2024. This decline has been primarily driven by the stabilization of global commodity prices, especially energy and food. However, core inflation remains elevated at 3.9%, reflecting continued domestic pressures, such as strong wage growth and expansionary fiscal policies that have fueled demand. Despite these challenges, disinflationary trends are expected to continue, though at a slower pace, as wage and pension increases outpace productivity growth. Key Considerations are:

Strengthening Monetary Policy Transmission Mechanisms: One of the major concerns for Bulgaria's inflation management is the weak transmission of European Central Bank (ECB) policy rates to domestic rates, particularly for household lending. Despite increases in the base rate by the Bulgarian National Bank (BNB) in line with ECB policy, the domestic market continues to experience weak pass-through effects. This weak transmission has led to excessive credit growth, especially in mortgages, with interest rates remaining relatively low compared to other EU countries. Addressing this issue is crucial to prevent excessive credit growth that could undermine monetary policy objectives, particularly as Bulgaria moves toward adopting the euro.

Enhancing Macroprudential Tools: Concerns over the rapid growth of mortgage credit, which has surged by 22% year-on-year as of early 2024, particularly in the context of rising house prices and low interest rates are essential to be considered. Elevated mortgage lending, along with a high preference for real estate investment, presents potential risks of real estate overheating. While the banking system remains well capitalized and the non-performing loans (NPL) ratio is relatively low, further strengthening Bulgaria's macroprudential framework to better manage risks associated with elevated mortgage credit growth is recommended. This includes the introduction of borrower-based measures to maintain asset quality and avoid the development of a house price-credit spiral.

These measures, coupled with the ongoing EU-driven regulatory changes, will be key to maintaining monetary stability in Bulgaria and preventing any long-term financial vulnerabilities, especially as the country gears up for eventual euro adoption. Careful management of credit growth and inflation expectations will be critical in achieving sustainable economic growth and meeting the EU's convergence criteria for euro adoption.

Investment Opportunities: Unlocking Bulgaria's Potential

Bulgaria's transformation into a modern, resilient economy hinge on strategic investments in key sectors such as green energy, digitalization, and infrastructure. These sectors are not only central to Bulgaria's long-term growth but also offer lucrative opportunities for investors. The country's integration into the EU provides access to significant funding and market opportunities, making it an attractive destination for investors looking for long-term growth aligned with sustainability and innovation.

Green Energy Transition: Investments in renewable energy projects, energy efficiency technologies, and emissions reduction initiatives offer substantial opportunities, particularly in light of Bulgaria's energy transition goals. The country is heavily dependent on coal, which remains a challenge for its green transition. However, the EU's financial backing, including funding through the Just Transition Fund, is helping phase out coal and promote renewable energy. The territorial Just Transition Plans will channel over 1% of GDP in EU funds to support the green transition, making this a critical area for investment. Additionally, fostering energy security by investing in renewable sources will be essential for reducing energy dependence and improving sustainability.

Digital Transformation: Bulgaria's ICT sector is rapidly growing, with notable opportunities in software development, artificial intelligence (AI), and digital infrastructure. The EU Recovery and Resilience Plan funds are providing much-needed support to expand the digital infrastructure and enhance the country's digital economy. The country's ability to bridge the digital skills gap through targeted education reforms is essential to fully capitalize on these opportunities. Investments in AI and digital tools could significantly boost Bulgaria's competitiveness in the global market .

Infrastructure and Logistics: Investment in transportation networks and regional connectivity is key to Bulgaria's development. The country's strategic location as a bridge between Europe and Asia makes it a critical hub for trade and logistics. Improving infrastructure will allow Bulgaria to better integrate into global value chains (GVCs), thus enhancing the flow of goods and knowledge across borders. Additionally, modernizing urban infrastructure to align with sustainable development goals is becoming increasingly important as Bulgaria works to ensure long-term resilience and economic growth.

Sustainable Tourism: With its rich cultural heritage, natural landscapes, and historical sites, Bulgaria has significant potential for diversifying its tourism offerings. Moving beyond traditional tourism, there is growing interest in eco-tourism, wellness tourism, and cultural heritage investments. These sectors align well with the EU's sustainability goals and provide opportunities for long-term, responsible investment. Developing these alternative forms of tourism can also help reduce seasonality and extend the economic benefits of tourism year-round.

In conclusion, Bulgaria's investment landscape is rich with opportunities, particularly in sectors that contribute to the green transition, digital transformation, infrastructure development, and sustainable tourism. The key to unlocking these opportunities lies in maintaining political stability, strengthening governance frameworks, and effectively utilizing EU funds to foster growth and innovation.

Governance and Structural Reforms: Foundations for Growth

Improving governance and combating corruption are essential for sustaining investor confidence and unlocking Bulgaria's economic potential. The country has made strides in recent years with judicial reforms, anti-corruption measures, and enhanced compliance mechanisms that address long-standing concerns. However, the implementation of these reforms remains critical for long-term success. Bulgaria's governance challenges are compounded by a perception of substantial corruption and weak rule of law, which continue to hinder economic growth despite efforts for improvement. It is noted that public procurement is an area particularly at risk for corruption, underscoring the need for continued reform and transparency. Reform Agenda:

Enhance Transparency in Public Procurement and SOE Governance: A critical area of reform is the transparency of public procurement and the governance of state-owned enterprises (SOEs), which play a significant role in the Bulgarian economy, particularly in sectors like energy and transportation. SOEs are less profitable than private firms, largely due to inefficiencies in management and governance. Furthermore, many SOEs face liquidity issues and fail to meet their short-term liabilities, posing fiscal risks that could undermine overall economic stability. Enhancing transparency and introducing stronger accountability measures within these entities will help reduce these risks and improve their economic contribution.

Strengthen Anti-Corruption Frameworks and Accelerate EU-Mandated Reforms to Unlock Additional Funding: Bulgaria's commitment to judicial reforms has been demonstrated by the 2023 amendments to the constitution, which aim to limit the power of the Prosecutor General and restructure the Supreme Judicial Council. These changes, along with improvements in the transparency of the regulatory selection process, have already contributed to progress in meeting EU requirements. The European Commission has recently closed its Cooperation and Verification Mechanism in recognition of these efforts. However, the implementation of key reforms—such as those related to anti-corruption efforts and asset recovery—has been delayed, potentially limiting Bulgaria's access to further EU funds. The swift implementation of these reforms is crucial to unlock additional financial support for Bulgaria's development and economic recovery.

Address Inefficiencies in Judicial Systems to Improve the Ease of Doing Business: Efficient and transparent judicial systems are foundational for attracting investment and facilitating business operations. While Bulgaria has introduced several important legal reforms—such as the 2023 whistleblower protection law and improvements in judicial human resources management—the full effectiveness of these reforms hinges on their timely and thorough implementation. Continued efforts to enhance judicial efficiency are vital, particularly in addressing high-level corruption cases, to improve the overall business climate and facilitate faster decision-making in commercial disputes.

Continued governance reforms and structural changes will not only address the immediate fiscal and economic challenges but will also position Bulgaria to better integrate into the European Union's economic framework and secure long-term growth and stability.

A Vision for Inclusive and Sustainable Growth

Bulgaria's path to sustained economic growth requires balancing fiscal prudence with strategic investments in human capital, infrastructure, and green energy. By addressing demographic challenges, fostering digital transformation, and improving governance, Bulgaria can position itself as a resilient and dynamic economy in the heart of Europe.

For investors, the message is clear: Bulgaria offers substantial opportunities across sectors integral to the global economy's future, from green energy to digital technologies. Aligning with the country's strategic priorities ensures not just

financial returns but also a contribution to a nation poised
for transformation.

Chapter (20)

Luxembourg: Shaping a Competitive, Resilient, and Sustainable Economic Landscape

Luxembourg, located in Western Europe, is a small, landlocked country with a population of approximately 655,000 people in 2024. The country covers an area of 2,586 square kilometres, making it one of the smallest countries in Europe. Luxembourg's economy is robust, with a projected GDP growth of 1.3% for 2024, following a contraction in 2023. This small yet wealthy nation is known for its financial sector, which plays a significant role in its economy, contributing to its high GDP per capita. Despite facing challenges such as a weakened real estate market and external demand pressures, Luxembourg's economy remains resilient due to its sound fiscal policies and high levels of government investment. It is forecasted that Luxembourg's GDP at €77.5 billion for 2024.

Luxembourg's economic narrative stands at a transformative juncture, characterized by challenges from global financial and geopolitical uncertainties alongside immense potential for innovation-driven growth. The 2024 IMF Article IV Consultation provides a comprehensive analysis of Luxembourg's current economic dynamics, fiscal challenges, and investment opportunities. This chapter explores Luxembourg's economic performance, fiscal policy landscape, and the investment climate, shedding light on structural reforms and strategic imperatives.

Economic Performance: Resilience Amidst Adjustment

Economic Trajectory

Luxembourg's economy contracted by 1.1% in 2023 due to a combination of weak external demand and a pronounced downturn in residential investment. Nominal GDP, however, saw a moderate increase, buoyed by wage growth of over 10%, reflecting the robust labor market and automatic wage indexation. The financial sector, construction, and transportation all experienced contractions, normalizing from high post-pandemic levels. GDP growth is forecasted to recover to 1.3% in 2024, with further strengthening to 2.9% by 2025 as external demand stabilizes and the impact of government support measures permeates the economy.

Despite these projections, the recovery remains fragile. Downside risks, including external supply shocks, geopolitical tensions, and a disorderly correction in asset prices, could dampen growth. Achieving long-term potential growth, estimated slightly above 2%, will depend on addressing supply-side constraints and reinforcing Luxembourg's competitive edge.

Inflation Trends

Inflationary pressures eased substantially in 2023, with headline inflation falling to 3.5%, driven by a reversal of earlier energy and food supply shocks. Core inflation, however, remains elevated at 4%, reflecting wage-driven cost pressures and base effects from administrative price measures. The trajectory suggests further moderation, with inflation expected to drop below 3% in 2024 before rebounding to 3.1% in 2025 as energy price controls expire. Maintaining this momentum toward the ECB's 2% target will require vigilance and carefully calibrated fiscal and monetary policies.

Labor Market Dynamics

Unemployment rose to 5.5% in 2023, reflecting a cooling labor market amid broader economic adjustments. Construction and manufacturing faced the steepest challenges, with vacancies declining by 36%. Skill mismatches, particularly in high-demand sectors like ICT and management, persist, complicating hiring efforts. Still, total employment grew by 1.3%, underscoring the resilience of the broader labor force. Enhancing labor market flexibility and addressing skill gaps will be pivotal for sustained productivity growth.

Fiscal Policy: Balancing Growth Support with Long-Term Stability

Debt and Deficit Dynamics

Luxembourg's fiscal strength remains a cornerstone of its AAA credit rating. The overall deficit widened to 1.3% of GDP in 2023, with public debt at a low 25.7% of GDP. However, projections indicate debt could rise to 31.4% by 2029 without structural adjustments. Fiscal policy is expected to remain moderately expansionary in 2024, with a focus on boosting housing demand and household purchasing power through tax adjustments and targeted measures.

While such measures are necessary to cushion the economic downturn, relying on permanent spending increases must be cautioned. Moving into 2025, as growth stabilizes, a contractionary fiscal stance will be essential to address medium-term pressures from aging demographics, rising healthcare costs, and climate transition investments.

Tax Reforms and Revenue Strategies

The newly elected government has committed to lowering corporate tax rates to align with the OECD average, enhancing Luxembourg's competitiveness. However, revenue loss risks must be mitigated through targeted measures. Recommendations regarding Luxembourg's tax reforms, emphasizing the need for careful design to maintain fiscal stability and competitiveness. Key aspects of these recommendations include:

Adjusting Tax Brackets for Inflation: Regular adjustments of tax brackets to account for inflation, ensuring that taxpayers are not unduly burdened as the cost-of-living rises is supported. However, it advises that such adjustments be implemented in a budget-neutral manner to prevent revenue losses.

Corporate Income Tax (CIT) Rate Reduction: It is noted that the intended reduction of the CIT rate could potentially lead to lower revenues without necessarily attracting new businesses. It suggests that any CIT rate cuts be carefully calibrated to avoid adverse fiscal impacts.

Streamlining Tax Expenditures: Reviewing and streamlining tax expenditures is recommended, such as interest rate deductibility, to enhance the efficiency and equity of the tax system.

Pension Reform: Given the projected rise in pension costs due to demographic pressures, early pension reform to ensure long-term sustainability and intergenerational equity is vital.

National Fiscal Framework: Luxembourg's intention to strengthen its national fiscal framework by complementing EU rules with a medium-term objective (MTO) is paramount. This approach aims to better anchor fiscal policy and maintain a credible commitment to the country's AAA credit rating.

In summary, it is recommended for Luxembourg's tax reforms focus on prudent fiscal management, ensuring that tax adjustments and reforms are carefully designed to avoid

revenue losses while maintaining economic competitiveness
and long-term fiscal sustainability.

Investment Landscape: Opportunities and Constraints

Green Economy Transition

As a leader in sustainable finance, Luxembourg is poised to
capitalize on its growing green bond market and burgeoning
opportunities in renewable energy infrastructure. The
government's commitment to climate transition is reflected
in its sustained public and private investments. However, the
continued reliance on fossil fuel subsidies and
underwhelming renewable capacity expansion threaten to
undermine these efforts. Investments in energy-efficient
infrastructure and a clearer roadmap for decarbonization are
imperative.

Digital Transformation

Luxembourg's strategic emphasis on innovation is central to
its economic agenda. Significant opportunities exist in AI,
advanced manufacturing, and financial technology,
supported by the National Digitalization Strategy. However,
persistent digital divides and skill shortages in frontier
technologies risk stalling progress. Public-private
partnerships and targeted workforce reskilling programs are
critical to overcoming these barriers.

Real Estate and Housing

Luxembourg's housing market underwent an orderly correction in 2023, with residential prices declining by 14.5%. While this rebalancing eases affordability concerns, construction activity has plummeted, with bankruptcies and layoffs signaling deeper sectoral challenges. Government measures, including expanded public housing projects and tax incentives, aim to revive the sector. Over the medium term, addressing structural imbalances will require a shift from demand-side interventions to supply-side solutions, such as densification initiatives and streamlined permitting processes.

Strategic Challenges and Opportunities

Structural Reforms

Luxembourg's productivity growth, averaging 0.3% since the global financial crisis, lags behind regional peers. Key reforms include:

Labor Market: Enhancing flexibility and addressing skill mismatches to boost labor mobility.

Public Administration: Streamlining regulations to reduce administrative bottlenecks and foster innovation.

Pensions: Early reforms to address demographic pressures, with aging-related costs projected to rise by 2 percentage points of GDP by 2040.

Financial Sector Resilience

Despite recent market volatility, Luxembourg's financial sector remains robust, with capital adequacy ratios above EU averages. However, rising non-performing loans (1.9% in 2023, up from 1.6% in 2022) and vulnerabilities in the real estate sector warrant attention. The introduction of sectoral systemic risk buffers and tighter loan-to-value (LTV) limits could mitigate these risks. Enhanced AML/CFT frameworks and cross-border collaboration are also crucial to safeguarding Luxembourg's position as a global financial hub.

Luxembourg: a compelling blend of stability, innovation and opportunity

Luxembourg's economic outlook is one of cautious optimism, driven by strategic reforms and targeted investments. Its commitment to fiscal discipline and sustainability, coupled with a focus on green and digital transformations, positions it as a resilient and innovative economy. However, navigating the complexities of global uncertainties and domestic structural imbalances requires nuanced and proactive policymaking. For investors, Luxembourg presents a compelling blend of stability, innovation, and opportunity in a rapidly evolving global landscape.

Chapter (21)

Croatia: A Strategic Economic and Investment Landscape in Transition

Croatia's Evolving Economic Landscape

Croatia, located in Southeastern Europe, is characterized by its diverse geography, with a long Adriatic coastline, mountainous regions, and fertile plains. It covers an area of approximately 56,594 square kilometres. The country's population stands at around 4 million people as of 2024, and it has a well-diversified economy with strong contributions from tourism, agriculture, and industrial sectors. For FY24, Croatia's nominal GDP is projected to reach approximately $88 billion.

Croatia, a rising star in the European Union, exemplifies a nation in transformation. Its post-pandemic economic trajectory, strategic investments in green and digital transitions, and adoption of structural reforms have placed it at the forefront of emerging opportunities in the eurozone. However, persistent challenges, including demographic shifts, skills mismatches, and subdued productivity, necessitate innovative policy interventions. The 2024 IMF

Article IV Consultation provides an in-depth analysis of Croatia's economic dynamics, highlighting key sectors poised for growth, fiscal discipline, and investment potential.

Enhanced Economic Dynamics

Sustained Growth with Emerging Challenges

Croatia's economic growth, forecasted at 3.4% in 2024, surpasses the eurozone average, positioning the country as a model of resilience. However, the sustainability of this growth hinges on addressing labor market inefficiencies and diversifying economic drivers beyond tourism and EU-backed investments.

Sectoral Contributions: Growth has been fueled by robust household consumption, public sector wage increases, and EU-funded investments, particularly in infrastructure and reconstruction projects following natural disasters. However, manufacturing and goods exports remain underwhelming, reflecting weak external demand from major trading partners.

Inflation Dynamics: Inflation has decelerated to 4.3% in May 2024, yet core inflation remains sticky at 4.6%, driven by rising wages and high tourism-related demand. Policymakers face the challenge of balancing inflationary pressures with the need to maintain real income growth and consumer confidence.

Labor Market Challenges: Unemployment stands at a low 5.6%, yet structural issues persist:

Demographic Pressures: An aging population and continued emigration exacerbate labor shortages.

Skills Mismatches: The education system must evolve to meet labor market needs, particularly in high-demand sectors like IT, healthcare, and renewable energy.

Foreign Workforce Integration: Recent reforms streamline work permits and integrate foreign workers to alleviate shortages.

Opportunities Amid Challenges

Croatia's growth story is underpinned by significant opportunities in eco-tourism, renewable energy, and digital innovation. Addressing structural challenges could unlock higher potential growth, while targeted reforms in productivity and regulatory efficiency will attract further investment.

Fiscal Policies: Balancing Expansion and Discipline

Strategic Debt Reduction and Deficit Management

Croatia's fiscal policy prioritizes sustainability. Public debt declined from 86.1% of GDP in 2020 to 63% in 2023, reflecting disciplined fiscal consolidation and robust GDP growth. Projections suggest further reduction to 55% by 2029, ensuring long-term fiscal credibility.

Tax Modernization for Sustainable Growth:

Property Tax Reform: Introducing a value-based property tax could enhance revenue streams and reduce distortions in the housing market caused by speculative investments. Modernizing cadastral systems by 2026 will support this effort.

Broadening the Tax Base: Aligning short-term rental income taxation with traditional property tax rates will curb speculative demand and stabilize the housing market. Further, reducing tax expenditures and exemptions can improve overall tax equity.

Green Taxation: Carbon pricing mechanisms and the removal of fossil fuel subsidies (estimated at 2% of GDP annually) will not only generate revenue but also support Croatia's climate goals.

Public Spending Efficiency:

Healthcare Reforms: Addressing arrears (0.7% of GDP in 2023) through co-payment systems and digitized health records can reduce costs and improve service delivery.

Pension System Adjustments: Aligning retirement ages, expanding second-pillar coverage, and indexing pensions to life expectancy are critical to ensuring sustainability amidst an aging population.

Public Sector Rationalization: Modernizing employment frameworks and enforcing attrition policies will optimize public workforce efficiency.

Enhancing Public Investment Management

The establishment of a dedicated Public Investment Management (PIM) unit at the Ministry of Finance signals Croatia's commitment to maximizing value for public investments. Incorporating climate resilience and green budgeting into investment decisions will align with broader EU goals.

Investment Horizons in Green and Digital Transformation

Green Transition: Leading the Sustainability Charge

Croatia's commitment to the EU's Fit-for-55 framework highlights its ambition to transition to a low-carbon economy. The National Energy and Climate Plan (NECP) outlines comprehensive goals for renewable energy adoption and energy efficiency improvements.

Energy Infrastructure: The renewable energy sector is ripe for investment, particularly in solar, wind, and hydroelectric projects. Energy storage and grid modernization initiatives will complement these efforts.

Carbon Pricing: A phased introduction of carbon taxes for sectors outside the EU Emissions Trading System (ETS) will drive decarbonization while generating public revenue.

Climate-Resilient Investments: Infrastructure projects integrating climate adaptation measures, such as flood defenses and urban cooling systems, align with EU resilience goals.

Digital Economy: Building the Foundations of Tomorrow

is a comprehensive strategy designed to facilitate the country's recovery from the COVID-19 pandemic, enhance economic resilience, and promote sustainable development. Aligned with the European Union's Recovery and Resilience Facility (RRF), the plan outlines a series of reforms and investments aimed at addressing structural challenges and fostering long-term growth. Key Components of Croatia's NRRP:

Economic Transformation:

Green Transition: Investments in renewable energy, energy efficiency, and climate change adaptation to support environmental sustainability.

Digital Transformation: Enhancing digital infrastructure, promoting digital skills, and supporting the digitalization of public services and businesses.

Public Administration and Judiciary:

Reforms to improve the efficiency and transparency of public administration and the judiciary system, thereby strengthening the rule of law and governance.

Education, Science, and Research:

Initiatives to improve access to quality education, promote research and innovation, and align educational outcomes with labor market needs.

Labor Market and Social Protection:

Measures to boost employment, enhance social protection systems, and support vulnerable groups, ensuring social cohesion and inclusion.

Health:

Investments aimed at improving the resilience, accessibility, and quality of healthcare services, including advancements in digital health solutions.

Building Reconstruction:

Focused efforts on the reconstruction and modernization of buildings, particularly in areas affected by natural disasters, to improve safety and energy efficiency.

Financial Allocation:

The NRRP is supported by €6.3 billion in grants from the EU's Recovery and Resilience Facility. Approximately 40.3% of the plan's funding is dedicated to climate objectives, while 20.4% is allocated to fostering the digital transition.

Implementation and Impact:

The plan comprises 146 investments and 76 reforms, with the goal of making Croatia's economy more sustainable, resilient, and better prepared for future challenges. By addressing key structural issues and investing in critical sectors, the NRRP aims to stimulate economic growth, create jobs, and enhance the quality of life for Croatian citizens.

For more detailed information, the European Commission
provides an overview of Croatia's recovery and resilience
plan.

Financial Sector Stability

Resilience Amid Global Tightening

Croatia's financial system demonstrates resilience, with high
liquidity buffers, robust capital ratios, and a well-capitalized
banking sector. Non-performing loans declined to 2.6% in
2023, reflecting economic stability.

Real Estate Dynamics:

Residential Market: Property prices, though stabilizing,
remain overvalued by 6%. Activating idle housing stock and
moderating tax incentives for short-term rentals will address
affordability challenges.

Commercial Real Estate: With limited exposure to
commercial real estate risks, banks remain insulated from
potential market corrections.

Macroprudential Measures

The gradual increase of counter-cyclical capital buffers
(CCyB) to 1.5% by June 2024 reflects proactive financial
regulation, ensuring preparedness for potential shocks.

Purpose of Gradual Increase

Proactive Risk Management: By increasing the CCyB
gradually to 1.5%, regulators are anticipating the potential
risks that might emerge from the economic cycle. This

ensures that banks are well-capitalized to handle any shocks from credit risk or asset price corrections.

Mitigating Financial Imbalances: Croatia has experienced strong credit growth and rising housing prices. Although these markets show signs of stabilization, the increase in CCyB prepares the financial system for any renewed momentum or overheating.

Strengthening Resilience: As the economy is entering a mature expansionary phase, the higher buffer rate ensures that financial institutions can withstand unexpected systemic disruptions without resorting to credit tightening, which could exacerbate economic stress.

Impact on Financial Institutions

Increased Capital Requirements: Banks need to hold additional equity to meet the buffer requirements. While this might temporarily constrain profitability or dividend distributions, it reduces systemic vulnerabilities.

Sustained Credit Supply: Despite higher capital requirements, Croatian banks are well-capitalized, and the phased buffer increase is unlikely to adversely affect lending. This reflects strong fundamentals in the banking sector.

Rationale Behind a Gradual Approach

- A gradual increase allows financial institutions time to adjust without creating sudden liquidity constraints.

- It signals a commitment to financial stability while avoiding abrupt changes that could disrupt market confidence.

Broader Financial Stability Measures

The report highlights that the counter-cyclical capital buffer is part of a broader macroprudential framework that includes:

- Monitoring household and corporate credit risks.

- Addressing vulnerabilities in the real estate market, particularly residential housing loans.

- Managing systemic risks linked to inter-company lending and exposure to commercial real estate.

The increase of the CCyB to 1.5% by mid-2024 exemplifies Croatia's proactive regulatory approach to fostering a resilient financial system. This measure ensures that the banking sector is equipped to support economic stability even in adverse conditions, reflecting prudent alignment with evolving economic risks and eurozone-wide regulatory best practices.

Structural Reforms: Unlocking Economic Potential

Labor Market Innovation

To counter labor shortages, Croatia is prioritizing coordinated policies:

Vocational Training: Programs aligning curricula with market demand aim to ease school-to-work transitions.

Foreign Worker Integration: Language training and social mentoring for foreign workers will support seamless integration.

Adult Learning: Customized learning solutions, especially in rural areas, aim to enhance workforce adaptability.

Productivity Revival

Boosting Croatia's stagnant productivity requires a multi-faceted approach:

Start-Up Ecosystem: Venture capital initiatives and regulatory reforms will support innovative businesses.

R&D Funding: Expanding public R&D expenditure and fostering public-private partnerships are crucial to driving technological advancements.

Investment Opportunities

Strategic Sectors for Growth

Croatia's unique position offers diverse opportunities:

Tourism Evolution: Shifting toward eco-tourism and high-value cultural heritage projects aligns with global trends.

Infrastructure Development: EU-backed investments in green transportation and digital connectivity present stable, long-term returns.

Healthcare Innovations: Telemedicine, biotech, and eldercare solutions cater to a growing aging population, creating lucrative niches.

ESG Alignment: A Global Investment Appeal

Croatia's policies align with global Environmental, Social, and Governance (ESG) priorities. Green energy projects, sustainable urban development, and digital inclusivity enhance its appeal to ESG-conscious investors.

Conclusion: Croatia's Promising Horizon

Croatia's journey reflects a nation adeptly balancing growth with sustainability. Its strategic focus on green energy, digital transformation, and fiscal discipline underscores its commitment to convergence with advanced European economies. For investors seeking high-growth opportunities in a stable, future-oriented environment, Croatia offers unparalleled potential in sectors poised for long-term success.

Chapter (22)

Lithuania: Navigating Challenges and Seizing Opportunities for a Resilient Economic Future

Lithuania, located in the Baltic region of Northern Europe, spans an area of approximately 65,300 square kilometres. As of 2024, the country has a population of about 2.7 million people. Following a mild contraction in 2023, Lithuania's economy is expected to recover in 2024, with real GDP growth projected at 2.4%. The nominal GDP for the year is estimated to be around €75.9 billion.

Emerging from a period of macroeconomic turbulence, Lithuania stands at a transformative juncture. The nation's capacity to navigate lingering structural challenges while embracing sustainable growth paths will define its economic trajectory in the years to come. Drawing on the IMF's 2024 Article IV Consultation, this chapter delves into Lithuania's economic performance, fiscal strategies, and investment opportunities. It also highlights reforms essential for achieving a vibrant and inclusive future.

Economic Performance: Recovery Amid Shifting Dynamics

Economic Trajectory: Resilience Against Headwinds

After weathering a shallow recession marked by a 0.3% contraction in 2023, Lithuania's economy is projected to grow by 2.4% in 2024, underpinned by robust private consumption, accelerating public investment fueled by EU funds, and a gradual rebound in external demand. By 2025, annual GDP growth is expected to stabilize at 2.2%, though this trajectory is constrained by demographic pressures, structural inefficiencies, and global economic fragmentation.

The long-term outlook, while positive, remains clouded by geopolitical tensions and unresolved domestic challenges. Critical sectors, such as education and healthcare, require substantial reform to sustain productivity and ensure convergence with euro area standards.

Inflation Trends: Strong Disinflationary Momentum

Lithuania's disinflation narrative is one of success amid adversity. Inflation, which peaked at a staggering 20% in 2022—double the euro area average—has since fallen below the regional average, reaching 1.2% in 2024. Key drivers include falling commodity prices, tighter monetary policy, and the gradual phase-out of energy subsidies.

Core inflation, however, remains persistently elevated at 2.9%, reflecting robust wage growth and sticky service prices. Policymakers project that inflation will stabilize around 2-

2.5% over the medium term, a level consistent with Lithuania's ongoing economic convergence.

Labor Market Dynamics: Strength and Challenges

The Lithuanian labor market remains robust but faces structural challenges. With unemployment projected at 7.3% in 2024, the market benefits from steady immigration—particularly from Ukraine—but struggles with regional disparities and skill mismatches. These issues constrain productivity, particularly in sectors requiring digital and technical expertise. Real wage growth, while boosting consumption, intensifies inflationary pressures, requiring balanced policy responses.

Fiscal Policy: Navigating Pressures with Prudence

Debt and Deficit Dynamics

Lithuania's public debt, projected at 38.1% of GDP in 2024, is among the lowest in the EU, offering fiscal flexibility to address emerging challenges. However, the fiscal deficit is set to expand to 1.6% of GDP in 2024, driven by increased defense spending, higher borrowing costs, and inflation-linked expenditures.

Defense remains a fiscal priority, with allocations exceeding 2.5% of GDP in 2023 and potentially rising to 3% in the coming years. Meanwhile, demographic pressures, particularly an aging population, could drive long-term expenditure needs to 10% of GDP by 2050 without decisive reforms.

Tax System and Reform Opportunities

Lithuania's tax structure, though competitive, offers significant room for optimization:

Corporate Taxation: Aligning Lithuania's corporate tax framework with EU norms through rationalized incentives and higher rates could generate an additional 1% of GDP.

Environmental Taxes: A carbon tax on fossil fuels could raise 1.5% of GDP, aligning economic incentives with green transition goals.

Property Tax Modernization: Expanding property tax coverage could yield revenues of up to 0.8% of GDP, easing reliance on labor taxation.

Reducing Tax Expenditures: Streamlining concessions, which currently account for 4.5% of GDP, would enhance equity and efficiency.

Recalibrating fiscal targets to maintain a strong structural balance will be essential for navigating external shocks while ensuring fiscal sustainability.

Investment Landscape: Opportunities in Transition

Green Economy: An Unfolding Opportunity

Lithuania's green transformation is a cornerstone of its investment strategy. Transitioning from fossil fuel reliance to renewables offers immense potential, particularly in energy-efficient infrastructure and offshore wind projects. However, challenges persist, including financing gaps and limited domestic expertise in green technologies.

Digital Innovation: A Rising Star

The fintech revolution has positioned Lithuania as a leader in digital finance. Supported by a robust AML/CFT framework, the nation has attracted global players, including Revolut Bank, which now accounts for 18% of the banking system's assets. Expanding this success to other digital sectors, including AI and blockchain, will require continued investment in digital infrastructure and skills development.

Financial Sector Resilience

Lithuania's banking sector remains a pillar of stability, with high profitability, low non-performing loan (NPL) ratios, and ample liquidity buffers. Macroprudential measures have mitigated risks, though segments like commercial real estate require vigilance. Continued vigilance against non-systemic risks, particularly in real estate, will safeguard financial stability.

Strategic Challenges and Opportunities

Structural Reforms: Building a Competitive Foundation

Addressing systemic inefficiencies is critical to Lithuania's future growth:

Education and Skills: Rationalizing the school network and expanding vocational training will address skill mismatches, a pressing concern in high-demand sectors like IT.

Pensions: Linking retirement age to longevity and integrating pensions into the general tax system can ensure fiscal sustainability while protecting low-income retirees.

Healthcare: Redirecting resources toward preventive care and streamlining hospital operations will improve health outcomes and cost efficiency.

Regional Development: Bridging the Divide

Investing in underdeveloped regions through infrastructure projects and targeted incentives can reduce disparities and unlock economic potential. Logistics and manufacturing sectors, particularly in border regions, offer untapped opportunities.

EU Integration: Unlocking Critical Funding

Lithuania's access to EU funds is a linchpin for its digital and green transitions. Ensuring compliance with governance standards and implementing judicial reforms will unlock the full potential of EU financing.

Lithuania's Path Forward

Lithuania's economic outlook is a delicate balance of optimism and caution. With its dynamic fintech sector, emerging green economy, and stable fiscal position, the nation offers promising opportunities for investors. However, success hinges on bold reforms and strategic investments that prioritize sustainability and inclusivity. By fostering innovation, enhancing productivity, and addressing structural inefficiencies, Lithuania is well-positioned to achieve a resilient and prosperous future.

Chapter (23)

Slovenia: Resilience in the Face of Adversity and Seizing Opportunities for a Sustainable Future

Slovenia, located in Central Europe, covers an area of approximately 20,273 square kilometres and has a population of around 2.1 million people in 2024. The country's economy is expected to grow by 2% in FY24, supported by higher domestic demand, including flood-related investment, and a recovery in real wages. Slovenia's nominal GDP is forecasted to reach approximately €66.9 billion in 2024.

Slovenia, a dynamic nation in the heart of Europe, continues to rise above global uncertainties, navigating its path through a complex economic landscape. The country has proven its resilience by overcoming the shocks from the pandemic, geopolitical tensions, and devastating floods. But as it continues its recovery, Slovenia is also laying the groundwork for an economically sustainable and prosperous future. With a focus on green growth, digital transformation, and structural reforms, Slovenia is well-positioned to harness emerging opportunities, while addressing long-term challenges such as aging demographics and rising public spending. This chapter delves deeper into Slovenia's economic trajectory, fiscal strategies, investment potential, and the regulatory and tax reforms that are driving the country's recovery and growth.

Economic Performance: Resilient Recovery Amid Complex Challenges

Economic Trajectory

Slovenia's economic performance over the past few years has been characterized by a blend of remarkable recovery and formidable obstacles. After contracting by 4.2% in 2020 due to the pandemic, Slovenia rebounded strongly in 2021 with a growth of 8.2%, one of the most impressive recoveries in Europe. However, global disruptions, notably the war in Ukraine and escalating energy prices, cast a shadow on the following year. By 2022, growth decelerated to 2.5%, with supply chain bottlenecks and energy price surges impacting both domestic demand and export activities. In 2023, the country faced an additional blow with severe flooding, which caused direct damage estimated at 5% of GDP and triggered large-scale emergency spending.

Despite these setbacks, Slovenia's economy is projected to recover in 2024, with GDP expected to grow by 2%. This growth is driven by increased domestic demand, particularly from flood-related investments, alongside a boost in private consumption as real wages begin to recover. As Slovenia's economy continues to stabilize, growth is projected to settle closer to its potential at 2.5% by 2025. This resilience demonstrates the country's capacity to adapt and overcome, providing a solid foundation for long-term prosperity.

Inflation and Labor Market Resilience

Slovenia, like many European economies, grappled with high inflation in 2022, reaching peaks of 8.8% due to global energy shocks. However, inflationary pressures have significantly eased in 2023. The IMF forecasts inflation to fall to 2.7% by the end of 2024, with core inflation cooling to 2% by 2025. This easing of inflation is driven by declining global energy prices, the successful implementation of tighter monetary policies, and falling food prices. For Slovenian households, this decline in inflationary pressures means a restoration of purchasing power, thus creating a more favorable environment for consumption-led growth.

In terms of the labor market, Slovenia continues to experience tight conditions, with the unemployment rate at a historical low of 3.7% in 2023. While labor shortages persist, particularly in construction, hospitality, and administrative services, Slovenia's approach to addressing these gaps by increasing foreign labor supply has yielded positive results. Over 90% of the increase in employment in 2023 came from foreign workers. This is a clear indication of Slovenia's capacity to attract the talent it needs to fuel its recovery. As the labor market remains constrained, nominal wages grew by nearly 10% in 2023, contributing to higher living standards and stronger domestic consumption.

Fiscal Policy: Navigating Fiscal Pressures and Ensuring Long-Term Sustainability

Managing Deficits and Public Debt

Slovenia's fiscal policy has been a crucial lever in responding to recent crises, including the pandemic and the floods. Despite these challenges, the fiscal deficit narrowed slightly to 2.5% of GDP in 2023, down from 3.0% in 2022. This is a positive outcome given the increased public expenditure due to the floods and other pandemic-related support measures. Public debt, which had risen significantly during the pandemic years, continued to decrease in 2023, falling to 69.2% of GDP. The government's prudent debt management, including the use of fiscal buffers accumulated during low-interest years, has helped keep Slovenia's debt profile manageable.

However, it is noticeable that Slovenia faces long-term fiscal pressures, primarily due to demographic shifts and rising public spending on health, pensions, and social services. The Further fiscal consolidation, aiming for a gradual reduction of the fiscal deficit to zero by 2026 is recommended, which would help bring public debt down below 60% of GDP. To achieve this goal, Slovenia must implement comprehensive structural reforms, especially in pension and healthcare systems, and continue to streamline public sector expenditure.

Tax and Regulatory Reforms

Slovenia's tax system remains one of the country's most significant structural challenges. The high tax wedge—particularly on labor—has been a barrier to attracting skilled foreign workers and boosting private sector growth. Reducing the labor tax burden and offsetting the loss in revenue by raising property and environmental taxes is recommended, as well as broadening the VAT base. This would not only help lower the tax wedge but would also support growth in high-value sectors such as technology and green industries.

In line with fiscal consolidation, Slovenia has introduced a temporary tax on bank assets from 2024 to 2028 to finance the flood-related expenditures. While this measure is necessary to address the immediate reconstruction needs, such taxes could dampen investor confidence and bank capital over time. The government should, therefore, allow this tax to lapse after its five-year term.

Investment Opportunities: Green Transformation and Technological Innovation

Green Economy and Climate Resilience

Slovenia has placed a strong emphasis on sustainability and climate resilience, with significant investments aimed at reducing carbon emissions and adapting to climate change. The floods of 2023 highlighted the urgent need for climate-adaptive infrastructure, and the government is channelling funds into flood prevention and climate-resilient rebuilding. Slovenia aims to increase its renewable energy share, with the goal of achieving 30–35% of its energy from renewables by 2030, up from 29% in 2023. This green transformation offers considerable investment opportunities, particularly in renewable energy infrastructure, energy storage, and climate-resilient construction.

In addition, Slovenia's commitment to the European Green Deal and its long-term carbon neutrality target places the country at the forefront of green investments in Europe. For investors, Slovenia represents an attractive destination for projects in offshore wind energy, sustainable agriculture, and green technology, with favorable policies and an increasing share of EU funds dedicated to green initiatives.

Digital Transformation and Innovation

Slovenia's digital economy is flourishing, driven by robust government support for innovation and digital infrastructure. The country is focusing on expanding its digital economy through investments in artificial intelligence (AI), automation, and digital services. As part of the EU-backed National Recovery and Resilience Plan, Slovenia has prioritized digital investments to boost its technological capabilities and productivity growth. Slovenia's well-developed human capital, coupled with its vibrant startup ecosystem, offers excellent opportunities for venture capital and private equity investments, particularly in sectors such as fintech, digital health, and smart manufacturing.

The country's emphasis on digitalizing public services, improving regulatory efficiency, and creating a more favorable business environment presents another layer of investment potential. As Slovenia accelerates its digital transformation, businesses in the tech space can expect to find a competitive edge in a highly skilled labor force and growing demand for cutting-edge technologies.

Structural Reforms: Strengthening Competitiveness and Ensuring Sustainable Growth

Key Reforms to Address Long-Term Challenges

The long-term growth trajectory of Slovenia hinges on structural reforms aimed at addressing key challenges. Population aging remains one of Slovenia's most pressing issues, as it places increasing strain on the pension system and healthcare. Reforms in pensions are recommended, such as linking the retirement age to life expectancy and increasing pension contributions, to ensure the sustainability of the system. Reforms in the public wage system, which has created barriers to recruitment in certain sectors, are also necessary to address labor shortages, particularly for skilled workers.

In terms of the labor market, Slovenia's education system has achieved notable success in producing a skilled workforce. However, there is still a mismatch between the skills available and those required by the rapidly evolving economy. The government's new labor market platform, which predicts future labor market needs, is a step in the right direction. By aligning education policies with labor market demands, Slovenia can ensure that it remains competitive and ready for the future.

Tax System Overhaul and Capital Market Development

Slovenia's tax system overhaul is a central component of the government's broader strategy to enhance the country's competitiveness, promote sustainable economic growth, and attract investment. The country's tax framework is currently facing significant challenges that hinder its full potential, particularly in terms of labor market efficiency and investment incentives. However, the ongoing reforms are aimed at reducing these barriers and streamlining the system to improve both the business environment and the fiscal balance.

Reducing the Labor Tax Wedge

One of the primary targets of Slovenia's tax reforms is to address the high labor tax wedge, which remains one of the highest in Europe. Substantial taxes on labor—particularly in the form of social security contributions—are seen as a significant obstacle to attracting highly skilled foreign workers and boosting domestic employment. A high tax burden on labor can reduce the competitiveness of Slovenia's economy, particularly in the eyes of multinational companies and investors looking to establish operations in the country.

The government has recognized this challenge and has signaled its intention to reduce the labor tax wedge. This would encourage greater participation in the labor market, especially from underrepresented groups, and foster higher productivity by incentivizing skill development and labor mobility. A reduction in the tax wedge could stimulate labor supply, increase disposable incomes, and provide a more attractive environment for employers and workers alike.

While this reform would lead to a short-term reduction in tax revenue, it is expected to generate medium-term economic benefits through increased labor force participation, higher income tax receipts from expanded employment, and a stronger overall economy.

Broadening the Tax Base and Improving Efficiency

In parallel with labor tax reductions, Slovenia is also working to modernize and streamline its tax administration. There is a need for a more efficient and transparent tax system to enhance fiscal discipline, reduce tax evasion, and ensure a fairer distribution of tax burdens. Slovenia's efforts to broaden the tax base through a more comprehensive tax system could include revising existing tax incentives, reducing the reliance on narrow revenue streams, and improving the compliance environment. The government is exploring options to increase property and environmental taxes, which could offset the loss of revenue from labor tax cuts and simultaneously promote environmental sustainability and climate goals. Broadening the VAT base and improving tax administration, particularly in areas like VAT collection and dealing with tax expenditures, will also be a key focus. Strengthening enforcement mechanisms and enhancing digital infrastructure within the tax authority will help improve compliance, reduce administrative costs, and make the tax system more predictable and investor-friendly.

Capital Market Development

While Slovenia's tax system is undergoing significant reforms, another crucial area for the country's economic growth lies in the development of its capital markets. Slovenia's capital markets are relatively shallow compared to other European countries, with limited options for financing and fewer opportunities for private investment. The relatively underdeveloped capital markets hinder the ability of domestic companies, particularly small and medium-sized enterprises (SMEs), to access financing. This is particularly problematic for sectors that are key to Slovenia's future—such as technology, green energy, and advanced manufacturing—where venture capital and private equity financing are often required to fuel growth and innovation.

The government has recognized these challenges and is actively pursuing a comprehensive capital market development strategy to unlock the potential of Slovenia's financial markets. This strategy, which spans until 2030, aims to deepen Slovenia's capital markets by increasing the availability of financing through both public and private channels. The government's focus on improving access to capital will help ensure that businesses, particularly in emerging sectors, have the funding they need to innovate and grow.

Private Equity and Venture Capital

In particular, private equity and venture capital markets present an underexploited opportunity in Slovenia. By fostering a more vibrant venture capital ecosystem, the government hopes to attract more investors and encourage domestic entrepreneurship. The country's highly educated workforce and its emphasis on research and development make it a strong contender for tech startups and innovation-driven businesses, but access to funding has historically been limited.

It is of critical importance to provide adequate incentives and regulatory frameworks to encourage private investment in these areas. Strengthening the financial sector by improving access to early-stage financing, establishing tax incentives for venture capital investments, and enhancing the regulatory environment for startups are crucial components of the capital market development strategy. Additionally, greater liquidity and transparency in the capital markets will encourage institutional investors, such as pension funds and insurance companies, to allocate more capital to Slovenia's growth sectors.

The government's strategy also involves deepening connections with international financial markets, improving the regulatory framework for capital markets, and simplifying the process for private and public companies to list on the Slovenian stock exchange. This would improve the overall attractiveness of Slovenia as a financial hub in Central Europe, boosting investor confidence and facilitating cross-border investments.

The Role of EU Funds in Capital Market Development

A key aspect of Slovenia's capital market strategy involves leveraging European Union (EU) funds, which have become an increasingly important source of investment for infrastructure, innovation, and environmental projects. Slovenia has already tapped into EU funding to support its recovery from the COVID-19 pandemic and the 2023 floods. Further EU funds could be channeled into initiatives designed to foster financial market development, such as improving financial literacy, creating funding mechanisms for green investments, and supporting startups in emerging industries.

As Slovenia progresses with its capital market reforms, the combination of tax incentives, an improved regulatory environment, and increased access to EU financing will help strengthen the investment landscape. For investors, this creates an opportunity to tap into a rapidly developing market with strong growth prospects in key sectors such as renewable energy, digital technologies, and advanced manufacturing.

Conclusion: A Resilient Slovenia Poised for a Sustainable Future

Slovenia's journey through recent economic challenges—ranging from the pandemic to geopolitical shocks and devastating floods—has proven the nation's resilience. The country's focus on fiscal consolidation, green transformation, and digital innovation is laying the foundation for future growth and prosperity. Slovenia offers compelling opportunities for investment, particularly in green technologies, digital infrastructure, and high-value manufacturing sectors. By implementing key structural reforms, including those in pensions, public wages, and labor markets, Slovenia will continue to adapt and thrive in an ever-evolving global economy.

For investors seeking stability, innovation, and sustainability, Slovenia presents a forward-thinking destination poised to unlock significant growth in the years to come. Through its combination of policy agility, sustainable development strategies, and skilled labor, Slovenia is well on its way to becoming a leader in Europe's green and digital transitions, providing a fertile ground for investment opportunities that will shape the future of the region.

Chapter (24)

Latvia: Shaping Resilience and Harnessing Potential for Sustainable Growth

Latvia, situated in the Baltic region of Northern Europe, spans an area of 64,589 square kilometres. The country's population is approximately 1.8 million in 2024. Following a contraction of 0.3% in 2023, Latvia's economy is projected to rebound, with real GDP growth expected to reach 1.7% in 2024. This recovery is underpinned by increased private consumption, stronger public investment, and improving external demand. Latvia's nominal GDP for FY24 is estimated to be approximately €42.4 billion.

Latvia is poised at a critical moment of transformation, emerging from economic contraction and grappling with the multifaceted pressures of geopolitical tensions, climate adaptation, and demographic transitions. The IMF's 2024 Article IV Consultation illuminates Latvia's economic landscape, highlighting paths toward stability, reform, and opportunity. This chapter delves into Latvia's economic, fiscal, and investment environment, outlining the challenges and strategies that shape its trajectory toward sustainable prosperity.

Economic Performance: Resilience Amid Complex Dynamics

Economic Trajectory

Latvia's economy, after a 0.3% contraction in 2023, is forecasted to grow by 1.7% in 2024 and 2.4% in 2025, bolstered by recovering private consumption, increased public investment, and stronger external demand. This recovery marks a cautious optimism, as medium-term growth stabilizes around 2.5% annually. Structural reforms, public investment, and a shift toward a greener, more digitalized economy underpin this outlook. Yet, challenges persist. High geopolitical risks, geoeconomic fragmentation, and external shocks could temper this recovery, while delays in public investments and reforms may inhibit productivity gains and long-term growth potential.

Inflation Trends

Latvia has made significant progress in combating inflation, with headline inflation dropping from its 2022 peak of 22.1% to near-zero levels in mid-2024, driven by falling energy and food prices. Core inflation, however, remains elevated at 3.3%, reflecting persistent wage growth and service sector price pressures. The IMF projects inflation to stabilize at the European Central Bank's 2% target by 2026, contingent on wage moderation and energy price stabilization.

Labor Market Dynamics

The labor market remains a bright spot, with unemployment steady at 6.5% in 2023, a historically low level for Latvia.

However, the imbalance between nominal wage growth (11.9% in 2023) and productivity remains a pressing concern. Addressing labor mismatches, improving regional employment opportunities, and enhancing workforce skills in critical sectors are paramount to unleashing Latvia's full labor market potential.

Fiscal Policy: Bridging Stability and Strategic Investment

Debt and Deficit Dynamics

Latvia faces medium-term fiscal pressures, with the ESA fiscal deficit projected to reach 2.9% of GDP in 2024 and public debt rising to 44.7%. While fiscal performance has been stronger than anticipated, long-term challenges from aging, defense expenditures, and the green transition necessitate decisive reforms. By 2029, fiscal consolidation will be essential to rebuild buffers and create space for targeted investments.

Tax Reform for Sustainability

Latvia's tax strategy is pivotal in addressing fiscal challenges. Recommended tax reforms are:

Expanding tax bases: Rationalizing corporate income tax (CIT) and personal income tax (PIT) by reducing the shadow economy.

Reforming property taxation: Aligning cadastral values with market prices to enhance equity and revenue generation.

Targeting inefficiencies: Phasing out fossil fuel subsidies and narrowing tax exemptions, which currently account for a high share of GDP relative to peers.

Improving enforcement: Strengthening compliance mechanisms to boost revenue without raising statutory rates.

These measures could yield significant fiscal savings while enhancing the equity and efficiency of Latvia's tax system.

Expenditure Rationalization

Latvia must also optimize public expenditure by:

Refining social support mechanisms: Shifting from broad subsidies to targeted assistance for vulnerable populations.

Enhancing public investment management: Prioritizing high-impact projects in infrastructure, healthcare, and digitalization to stimulate growth.

Streamlining government operations: Consolidating spending in areas like goods and services and reforming public sector wages to reflect productivity.

Investment Landscape: Catalyzing Growth and Innovation

Green Economy

Latvia's commitment to sustainability creates vast opportunities in renewable energy, energy-efficient infrastructure, and green technologies. Accelerating the adoption of the National Energy and Climate Plan (NECP) and expediting investments under the Recovery and Resilience Facility are critical to achieving climate goals and reducing reliance on fossil fuels. Strategic priorities include expanding renewable energy capacity, modernizing electric grids, and enhancing energy security.

Digital Transformation

Latvia's digital strategy is a cornerstone for innovation-driven growth. Investments in artificial intelligence, digital infrastructure, and e-governance can bolster Latvia's position as a regional leader in technology. Yet, closing the digital divide across regions and upskilling the workforce are essential to fully leverage these opportunities.

Financial Sector Stability

Latvia's banking sector has weathered recent shocks, supported by strong capital adequacy and liquidity. However, vulnerabilities in the real estate market and high household debt levels tied to variable-rate loans require careful monitoring. Mitigating cybersecurity risks and aligning credit allocation with market needs are critical to ensuring long-term financial resilience.

Strategic Challenges and Pathways to Reform

Structural Reforms

Latvia must address systemic inefficiencies to unlock its economic potential:

Enhancing governance: Tackling corruption and strengthening regulatory frameworks to improve the business environment and attract foreign investment.

Boosting productivity: Facilitating private sector innovation through competition and reduced state-owned enterprise dominance.

Revitalizing labor supply: Expanding vocational training and STEM education to bridge skills gaps and adapt to emerging industries.

EU Integration

Leveraging €2 billion in EU Recovery and Resilience Facility funds is pivotal for Latvia's development. Effective governance, project implementation, and alignment with EU priorities are prerequisites for maximizing the impact of these resources.

Addressing Regional Disparities

Reducing regional inequalities through targeted incentives and infrastructure investment can unlock untapped economic potential. Investments in manufacturing, logistics, and digital connectivity in underdeveloped areas are critical to achieving balanced growth.

Latvia's Vision for a Sustainable Future

Latvia's journey toward economic resilience and sustainable growth hinges on its ability to balance fiscal discipline with strategic investments in innovation, inclusion, and sustainability. Opportunities in the green economy, digital transformation, and regional integration offer promising avenues for growth. However, realizing these ambitions requires unwavering commitment to reforms, robust governance, and policy predictability. For investors, Latvia presents a compelling mix of emerging opportunities tempered by the challenges of navigating a complex regulatory and fiscal environment. Through deliberate action and strategic vision, Latvia can chart a path toward a resilient, inclusive, and sustainable economic future.

Chapter (25)

Estonia: A Thriving Digital and Green Economic Frontier in Transition

Estonia, located in Northern Europe, covers an area of 45,227 square kilometres. The country's population is approximately 1.3 million people in 2024. Despite the ongoing challenges, such as weak productivity growth and high input costs, Estonia's nominal GDP for FY24 is projected at €38.8 billion.

Estonia stands as a vibrant example of resilience and transformation, where the digital frontier meets sustainable growth ambitions. A nation long celebrated for its technological innovation, Estonia is now pivoting towards harnessing its digital expertise to overcome economic challenges and unlock new avenues of growth. Guided by insights from the IMF's 2024 Article IV Consultation, this chapter explores Estonia's evolving economic landscape, fiscal management strategies, and burgeoning investment opportunities. Through its dynamic trajectory, Estonia exemplifies a small but ambitious nation redefining its role in a rapidly changing global economy.

Economic Performance: Resilience Amid Structural Shifts

Estonia's economic journey is a testament to the country's adaptability in the face of adversity. Recent years have seen significant economic turbulence, but Estonia's inherent strengths in digital transformation, fiscal discipline, and innovation continue to offer paths for recovery and future growth.

Economic Trajectory

The Estonian economy contracted by 3.0% in 2023, extending a recessionary trend marked by global uncertainty and challenges in the real economy. Nevertheless, signs of recovery are emerging. In 2024, GDP is projected to return to modest growth at -0.5%, with a more robust expansion of 2.2% in 2025. This growth is expected to be driven by stronger external demand and renewed domestic investments. It is anticipated that Estonia's export sector, once hampered by external shocks and competitive pressures, will find new momentum as demand from key trading partners like Finland and Sweden gradually strengthens.

Inflation Trends

Inflationary pressures, which peaked at a staggering 25% in 2022, moderated significantly in 2023 to 9.1%. While energy prices and supply chain disruptions have eased, VAT hikes and continued wage growth may sustain inflationary pressures into 2024, with a projected inflation rate of 3.8%. These dynamics underscore the delicate balance Estonia must strike in managing inflation while pursuing its broader fiscal and economic goals.

Labor Market Dynamics

Estonia's labor market has demonstrated resilience, despite rising unemployment, which reached 8.4% in 2024. Notably, the ICT sector and public services continue to absorb labor, with integration of Ukrainian refugees offering additional buffer against the downturns in manufacturing and construction. The country's strategic focus on education, training, and workforce flexibility remains key to counteracting the impact of structural unemployment and evolving labor market demands.

Fiscal Management: Balancing Stability and Ambition

Estonia has long been recognized for its fiscal prudence, boasting one of the lowest debt-to-GDP ratios in the European Union. This provides the country with significant fiscal space to weather current economic challenges and invest in long-term transformation.

Fiscal Discipline and Strategic Reforms

Estonia's fiscal management remains disciplined, even in the face of rising expenditure on defense, social programs, and green initiatives. Public debt, projected at 23% of GDP in 2024, is expected to rise to 34% by 2029, as the country continues to grapple with fiscal deficits. However, Estonia's approach to debt remains manageable due to the low starting

point, robust financial systems, and steady economic growth
projections.

Fiscal Innovations

Estonia's innovative approach to fiscal management includes
revenue-enhancing measures, such as the increase in VAT
and planned car registration taxes, which help finance critical
defense and green transformation projects. Structural
reforms are underway, targeting inefficiencies in public
spending while maintaining fiscal sustainability. These
include streamlined government programs, efficiency audits,
and the introduction of more rigorous means-testing for
social benefits.

Taxation Reform

A key feature of Estonia's economic strategy is its
competitive tax system, which emphasizes low corporate and
property taxes to attract investment. Expanding the tax base
through property taxation reforms and recalibrating income
taxes is recommended to ensure that they remain
progressive. These tax reforms are poised to address future
fiscal pressures while ensuring that Estonia maintains an
attractive environment for investors.

Pioneering Investment Opportunities: Green and Digital Frontiers

Estonia's commitment to both sustainability and
technological innovation positions the country as a fertile
ground for transformative investments. Anchored in its
digital ecosystem and forward-looking green policies,

Estonia offers unique opportunities for investors seeking to make an impact in the global market.

Green Economy Leadership

Estonia's climate ambitions are set on achieving carbon neutrality by 2050, though this goal faces significant challenges. A major aspect of the green transition involves the phase-out of oil shale, a historically significant but environmentally unsustainable energy source. The government is channeling investments into renewable energy, particularly offshore wind farms and solar energy projects, as part of its commitment to the European Union's climate goals.

Investment Hotspots

The renewable energy sector, especially offshore wind and solar, stands as one of the most promising growth sectors for Estonia. Public-private partnerships, supported by favorable regulatory frameworks and EU funding, create fertile ground for green technology investments. Estonia is also focused on enhancing energy efficiency across sectors such as transportation and construction, creating additional opportunities for sustainable investments.

Digital Transformation

Estonia has long been a pioneer in digital governance, with initiatives like its e-residency program, advanced IT infrastructure, and a thriving start-up ecosystem. The country is home to some of the most innovative digital enterprises in Europe, particularly in the fields of artificial intelligence (AI), health-tech, and smart manufacturing.

Emerging Sectors

Artificial intelligence, biotechnology, and smart manufacturing are poised for significant expansion. Estonia's robust venture capital ecosystem, combined with a skilled workforce and forward-thinking policies, provides a fertile environment for scaling up digital enterprises. These sectors are set to become key drivers of Estonia's economic growth, attracting both domestic and international investors.

Financial Resilience: Stability Amid Challenges

Estonia's financial sector remains a cornerstone of its economic resilience. Despite challenges, particularly in the commercial real estate sector, the country's banking system remains solid, with substantial capital buffers ensuring stability in the face of external shocks.

Banking Stability

Estonian banks' Common Equity Tier 1 (CET1) ratios have shown a downward trend, falling from over 40% in 2014 to approximately 21.5% in recent years. While this decline is notable, the CET1 ratios remain above the regulatory minimum, signaling that capital buffers are still sufficient to weather economic shocks. However, the concentration of real estate loans in bank portfolios requires vigilance, especially as real estate markets face volatility.

Macroprudential Vigilance

The Estonian central bank has implemented measures such as a 15% risk-weight floor on mortgage loans to mitigate potential risks in the housing market. Furthermore, the country's tight credit standards reflect proactive risk management strategies aimed at ensuring the stability of its financial system during uncertain economic times.

Navigating Strategic Challenges and Opportunities

Estonia faces a dual challenge: addressing internal structural issues while seizing opportunities for innovation and growth. Strategic investments in key areas such as digital transformation, green technology, and industrial modernization will be essential to overcoming these challenges and ensuring long-term prosperity.

Addressing Structural Pressures

Demographic shifts, particularly an aging population, coupled with rising structural unemployment, necessitate focused policy measures to incentivize labor market participation. Estonia's future workforce policies should aim at attracting skilled immigrants, promoting upskilling and reskilling programs, and reducing gender inequalities in the labor market.

Competitiveness and Innovation

Estonia's loss of export market shares highlights the need for innovation and diversification. To regain its competitive edge, Estonia must prioritize investments in productivity-enhancing technologies, particularly in the digital and green sectors. Innovation-driven growth, underpinned by robust

R&D and digital adoption, is vital for Estonia to maintain its position as a regional leader.

Strategic Investment Sectors

Estonia's forward-looking policies prioritize sustainability, inclusivity, and technological innovation, creating vibrant opportunities for strategic investments.

Renewable Energy: Offshore wind and solar energy projects lead Estonia's green transition, bolstered by EU funding and public-private partnerships.

Health-Tech and Biotechnology: With an aging population, Estonia's investments in telemedicine and biotech present lucrative opportunities for collaboration between the public and private sectors.

Advanced Manufacturing: Estonia's push towards automation in manufacturing aligns with broader EU objectives, making it a hub for industrial modernization.

Estonia's Path to Sustainable Growth

Estonia's economic journey underscores its resilience and adaptability. As the country transitions from a period of economic turbulence to a future of sustainable growth, its strategic focus on green and digital innovation will define its next chapter. Investors seeking transformative opportunities will find a promising landscape in Estonia, where creativity and pragmatism come together to lay the foundation for enduring success.

This chapter offers a comprehensive view of Estonia's economic narrative, providing insights for stakeholders eager to navigate and invest in one of Europe's most innovative and forward-thinking economies. Through its unwavering commitment to digital leadership and sustainability, Estonia is poised to emerge as a key player in the global economy, offering ample investment opportunities for the future.

Chapter (26)

Cyprus: A Dynamic Economy in Transition – Harnessing Resilience and Opportunities

Cyprus, an island nation in the eastern Mediterranean, covers an area of approximately 9,251 square kilometres. With a population estimated at about 1.23 million people in 2024, Cyprus has a small yet dynamic economy. The country's nominal GDP for FY24 is projected to reach €31.7 billion, with real GDP growth forecasted at 2.6%.

Cyprus's economy is a testament to adaptability and forward-thinking policies, weathering global shocks while fostering robust growth. The 2024 IMF Article IV Consultation report underscores the nation's resilience, driven by strategic investments, structural reforms, and fiscal prudence. This chapter offers an expanded exploration of Cyprus's economic journey, the investment potential it unlocks, and the regulatory and tax landscape shaping its future.

Resilience Amid Challenges

Cyprus stands as a beacon of resilience in a turbulent global economic landscape, showcasing the power of strategic adaptation. Amidst the lingering effects of the pandemic, geopolitical shocks such as the war in Ukraine, and energy market volatility, the Cypriot economy has maintained momentum. Growth moderated to 2.5% in 2023, but this pace outperformed the euro area average, highlighting the island's economic dynamism. Cyprus growth catalysts are:

Sectoral Strengths: A recovery in tourism, the ascendancy of Information and communication technology (ICT) services, and robust financial activities are key drivers. Tourism arrivals rebounded to near-record levels in 2023, fueled by diversification into markets like Israel and the Middle East, offsetting losses from Russia.

Inflation Stability: Headline inflation declined to below 2% in 2023 due to falling energy prices and tight monetary policy. Core inflation, although stickier, was contained at 2.5%.

Labor Market Dynamics: Unemployment dropped to a historic low of 5.9%, underscoring the vitality of the job market. However, labor shortages in key sectors signal skill mismatches, creating both challenges and opportunities for reforms.

Despite a challenging external environment, the outlook remains positive, with growth projected at 2.6% in 2024 and an acceleration to 3% in the medium term. This stability hinges on robust FDI inflows, EU-funded Recovery and Resilience Plan (RRP) initiatives, and ongoing structural reforms.

Fiscal Landscape: Consolidation for a Sustainable Future

Cyprus's fiscal achievements stand out in Europe, with public debt declining sharply from its post-2013 crisis peak. In 2023, debt fell to 77.3% of GDP, cementing the nation's reputation for fiscal discipline. Primary surpluses, robust revenue generation, and strategic fiscal management are the cornerstones of this success.

Fiscal Challenges and Reform Opportunities:

Debt Reduction Priorities: Fiscal policy is centered on reducing public debt to below 60% of GDP by 2027, creating buffers against future shocks. Maintaining primary surpluses of around 4% of GDP is critical to achieving this goal.

Targeted Expenditure: Investments in infrastructure and green energy are prioritized, while temporary measures like electricity subsidies and VAT exemptions are being phased out. Controlling the public sector wage bill is a vital reform area.

Long-Term Pressures: Demographic trends and climate commitments are set to increase public spending by 2.5% of GDP by 2030. Careful fiscal planning to address these pressures while preserving Cyprus's social safety nets.

Financial Stability and Sectoral Resilience

Cyprus's banking and financial sector has emerged stronger, with capital and liquidity buffers exceeding regulatory requirements. However, challenges remain, particularly in addressing legacy non-performing loans (NPLs) and managing real estate-related risks. Key insights are:

Banking Sector Health: Cyprus's banks are well-positioned to withstand macroeconomic shocks, with stress tests indicating resilience. Loan renegotiations have increased, reflecting proactive risk management.

Real Estate Vigilance: The property market remains buoyant, driven by foreign demand, yet systemic risks persist. With two-thirds of loans secured by real estate, ongoing regulatory vigilance is essential.

Legacy NPL Resolution: Cyprus's ambitious climate goals present a dual challenge and opportunity. The nation seeks to achieve climate neutrality by 2050, with interim goals including a 32% reduction in non-EU Emissions Trading System (ETS) sector emissions by 2030. This transition offers fertile ground for investors in green technology, renewable energy, and sustainable infrastructure. Investments highlights are:

Renewable Energy: Expanding solar, wind, and energy storage capacities is central to Cyprus's energy strategy. The delayed LNG terminal, expected to be operational by 2025, will further enhance energy diversification.

Green Taxation and Carbon Pricing: Broadening the carbon tax scope to all non-ETS sectors, coupled with targeted support for vulnerable households is vital. This approach balances fiscal goals with equity concerns.

Adaptation Measures: With rising temperatures and sea levels, investments in climate resilience, such as coastal protection and water resource management, are critical.

Regulatory and Tax Framework: A Strategic Reset

Cyprus is aligning its regulatory environment with international best practices, focusing on anti-money laundering (AML) and combating financing of terrorism (CFT). A single supervisory framework for administrative services and enhanced oversight of the real estate sector are key priorities.

Tax System Overhaul

The ongoing review of Cyprus's tax system aims to modernize it for the digital age while ensuring alignment with the EU's tax directives. Green taxation and a fairer income tax regime are at the forefront of reforms.

Taxation and Revenue Enhancements

Green taxation, aligned with climate objectives, is a pivotal reform. Coupled with the EU's 15% minimum corporate income tax for multinationals, Cyprus is overhauling its tax regime to ensure fairness, efficiency, and sustainability. VAT system optimization and enhanced compliance mechanisms further boost revenue potential.

Investment Climate: Unlocking Cyprus's Potential

Cyprus's investment appeal lies in its strategic location as a gateway between Europe, the Middle East, and Africa, bolstered by EU membership, a skilled workforce, and a business-friendly regulatory framework. There are several sectoral opportunities where the island nation excels, while also identifying areas for reform and innovation to enhance its attractiveness to global investors is required.

Information and Communication Technology (ICT): Building a Regional Tech Hub

Cyprus is rapidly establishing itself as a premier destination for ICT investments. The government's focus on digital transformation is supported by significant advancements in infrastructure, including nationwide 5G coverage and an expanding fiber-optic network. Key initiatives aim to position Cyprus as a leader in artificial intelligence (AI), blockchain, and cybersecurity.

Supportive Policy Environment: National digital strategies prioritize innovation, data protection, and e-government services. The Recovery and Resilience Plan (RRP) includes €282 million allocated for digital transformation projects, signaling robust state support for ICT growth.

Emerging Opportunities: Growth in fintech, cybersecurity, and cloud computing services is attracting global companies. The island's integration into the EU's Digital Single Market further enhances its potential as a regional ICT hub.

Talent Development: Addressing skill shortages remains a priority, with reforms in education to promote STEM fields and targeted initiatives to upskill workers in emerging technologies.

Tourism and Real Estate: A Pillar of Economic Growth

Tourism remains a cornerstone of Cyprus's economy, with a remarkable post-pandemic recovery fueled by a strategic pivot to new markets. The country's idyllic Mediterranean setting, coupled with its rich cultural heritage, makes it a perennial favorite among tourists and real estate investors alike.

Tourism Recovery and Diversification: While traditional markets such as Russia faced disruptions, Cyprus successfully attracted visitors from the Middle East, Israel, and Europe. New tourism initiatives emphasize sustainable travel, eco-tourism, and the promotion of lesser-known regions.

Real Estate Investments: The property market is buoyed by demand from foreign buyers, particularly for high-end residences and commercial properties. Non-EU investors account for a significant portion of this activity, with attractive visa and residency schemes as key incentives.

Infrastructure Development: The government has prioritized investment in transport, urban regeneration, and smart city projects, further boosting the appeal of the real estate sector.

Professional Services: A Thriving Sector with Global Reach

Cyprus's robust legal, accounting, and financial services ecosystem is a testament to its adaptability and alignment with international standards. These services continue to attract multinational corporations and high-net-worth individuals.

Legal and Accounting Expertise: The island is a preferred jurisdiction for corporate structuring, tax planning, and cross-border legal advisory services, thanks to its competitive tax regime and compliance with EU regulations.

Financial Services: A diversified banking sector, coupled with regulatory alignment with the EU and OECD standards, strengthens Cyprus's reputation as a financial hub. Emerging trends include the growth of green finance and ESG-aligned investment opportunities.

AML/CFT Improvements: Strengthened anti-money laundering frameworks enhance Cyprus's standing as a credible and secure destination for professional services.

Addressing Challenges: Innovation and Reform

While Cyprus has made impressive strides in economic resilience and investment attractiveness, several challenges remain that necessitate targeted interventions and innovative strategies to sustain growth and competitiveness. These include addressing labor market dynamics, streamlining governance and bureaucracy, and mitigating geopolitical and external risks.

Labor Market Pressures: Bridging Gaps and Building Skills

The tight labor market, with unemployment at historic lows, underscores Cyprus's economic vitality but also reveals critical inefficiencies. A pronounced mismatch between available jobs and workforce skills is evident, particularly in high-demand sectors such as ICT, tourism, and healthcare.

Education System Overhaul

Aligning educational outcomes with labor market needs is essential. The government is focusing on modernizing curricula to include more digital and technical skills, increasing STEM graduates, and promoting vocational training.

Digital Readiness: Investment in digital education and infrastructure aims to prepare the younger workforce for technology-driven industries.

Upskilling Initiatives: Programs targeting adult workers in declining industries will help transition them into growing sectors like renewable energy and digital services.

Labor Force Expansion

The labor shortages in sectors like tourism and construction necessitate strategic policies to attract foreign talent while addressing underutilized segments of the domestic workforce.

Gender and Youth Participation: Measures to increase participation rates among women and young people, including childcare support and career counseling, are critical.

Immigration Reforms: Streamlined procedures for work permits, particularly for high-skilled workers, aim to attract global talent.

Activation Policies: Stricter requirements for job seekers, coupled with incentives for private-sector job creation, are designed to reduce structural unemployment and enhance labor force productivity.

Governance and Bureaucratic Efficiency: Creating a Business-Friendly Environment

Cyprus has made progress in governance reforms, but inefficiencies in bureaucracy and judicial processes continue to deter investment. Addressing these systemic issues is critical to fostering a more transparent and predictable business environment.

Judicial System Enhancements:

Ongoing reforms aim to reduce case backlogs and accelerate dispute resolution.

Digitization of Courts: Investments in e-justice platforms and digital case management systems are expected to significantly reduce delays and increase transparency.

Specialized Courts: The establishment of commercial courts focuses on expediting business-related disputes, improving confidence among investors.

Regulatory Streamlining: Simplifying business processes is a priority to reduce administrative burdens on companies.

One-Stop-Shop Services: Consolidated service centers for business registration and compliance are being enhanced to minimize red tape.

Regulatory Predictability: Efforts to harmonize regional and federal regulatory frameworks aim to provide clarity and stability to investors.

Transparency and Anti-Corruption: Strengthened anti-corruption frameworks and improved oversight mechanisms are integral to boosting public trust and international credibility.

AML/CFT Improvements: Implementation of the MONEYVAL recommendations continues, with a focus on addressing vulnerabilities in the real estate sector and administrative services.

Geopolitical and External Risks: Building Resilience and Diversification

As a small open economy, Cyprus remains highly vulnerable to external shocks, particularly those affecting its key sectors like tourism and professional services. Proactive measures to diversify economic reliance and build resilience are essential.

Tourism Diversification: While the rebound in tourism has been robust, over-reliance on specific markets, such as the EU and Israel, leaves Cyprus exposed to geopolitical tensions and economic slowdowns in these regions.

Expanding Source Markets: Strategic marketing efforts are targeting Asia and the Americas to attract a more diverse pool of tourists.

Sustainable Tourism Development: Investments in eco-tourism and off-season travel options aim to stabilize revenue streams.

Trade and Investment Diversification: Cyprus's export profile, heavily skewed towards services, is being balanced with initiatives to boost manufacturing and high-value goods production.

Strategic Sectors: Renewable energy and pharmaceuticals are being prioritized for export expansion.

Regional Trade Alliances: Strengthening ties with non-EU partners in the Middle East and Africa is a focus area to mitigate regional geopolitical risks.

Climate and Energy Security: Cyprus is vulnerable to climate-related risks, including rising sea levels and extreme weather, which threaten infrastructure and economic stability.

Renewable Energy Investments: Accelerating the deployment of solar, wind, and energy storage systems reduces reliance on volatile energy imports.

Climate Adaptation Strategies: Policies to safeguard coastal areas and manage water resources are being implemented to protect critical assets.

Cyprus recognizes that overcoming these challenges requires bold reforms and sustained innovation. By addressing labor market inefficiencies, streamlining governance, and diversifying economic dependencies, the nation is positioning itself as a resilient and adaptive economy. These efforts are critical not only for mitigating risks but also for unlocking new growth opportunities in an increasingly competitive global landscape.

Key Messages for Investors

Cyprus presents a compelling case for investment, blending resilience with significant growth potential. Its transition toward a greener and more digital economy, backed by EU funding and national reforms, creates opportunities across multiple sectors.

Sectoral Opportunities: ICT, green energy, tourism, and professional services are poised for growth, underpinned by government and EU support.

Strategic Alignments: Investors aligning with Cyprus's RRP goals and climate transition agenda will find favorable policies and incentives.

Local Partnerships: Collaborating with Cypriot entities can help navigate regulatory complexities and unlock market-specific insights.

Sustainability and Innovation: Green finance and digital solutions are integral to Cyprus's long-term strategy, offering investors avenues to contribute to and benefit from sustainable development.

By embracing innovation, fostering resilience, and leveraging its strategic location, Cyprus is well-positioned to attract global investors and solidify its status as a hub for sustainable growth and innovation.

Conclusion: Seizing the Momentum

Cyprus is at a critical juncture, where strategic investments can unlock significant economic potential. As the nation continues its green and digital transitions, it offers a unique opportunity for stakeholders to align with its long-term growth trajectory. With robust reforms and a forward-looking vision, Cyprus is poised to be a leader in Europe's evolving economic landscape.

Chapter (27)

Malta: Navigating Growth Amid Economic Resilience and Fiscal Challenges

Malta, located in the Mediterranean Sea, is a small island nation with a total area of 316 square kilometres. It has a population of approximately 0.52 million people as of 2022. The country's economy has been resilient, with real GDP growth forecasted at 5.1% for FY24. In 2022, its nominal GDP was recorded at around 17.5 billion Euros, with per capita income of approximately 33,496 euros.

Malta's economy stands at a pivotal crossroads, resilient in the face of significant challenges yet poised for transformative growth in an increasingly complex global landscape. As the Mediterranean nation recovers from the pandemic, contends with the ramifications of the Russia-Ukraine conflict, and grapples with energy price fluctuations, its economic trajectory offers a story of remarkable recovery, ongoing fiscal struggles, and evolving opportunities in green and digital innovation. This chapter takes an in-depth look at Malta's economic performance, fiscal policy strategies, investment climate, and the structural reforms that will be essential in realizing the country's long-term aspirations.

Economic Performance: Resilient Growth Amidst Persistent Pressures

Economic Trajectory Malta's economic recovery has been nothing short of impressive, defying the global headwinds that have hindered many other economies. After the sharp contraction of 2020, Malta's real GDP growth surged by 12.6% in 2021, followed by a solid 8.2% expansion in 2022. The growth was not just a rebound but a testament to Malta's ability to adapt, with the government's robust fiscal response, strong consumer demand, and an influx of migrant labor helping to maintain momentum. By 2023, the economy continued to expand at 6.2%, one of the highest rates in Europe, despite global economic slowdown. However, as pent-up demand from the pandemic fades and external pressures mount, growth is expected to moderate to 5% in 2024, reflecting a return to a more sustainable pace.

Looking further ahead, Malta's medium-term growth prospects remain positive but less buoyant. With global growth expectations subdued and local infrastructure and capacity constraints beginning to show, Malta's potential growth rate is expected to decline from pre-pandemic highs of 7% to a more modest 3.5% over the coming years. This reflects both structural limits, such as skill mismatches in the labor market and underdeveloped infrastructure, as well as external risks stemming from geopolitical tensions and slower European growth. Still, Malta's per capita income is forecasted to continue outpacing the euro area average, narrowing the income gap from 19% in 2022 to 11% by 2030.

Inflation Trends Despite the resilience of Malta's growth, inflationary pressures remain a critical concern. At the height of the energy crisis in late 2022, inflation spiked to 7.5%, driven by surging energy costs and global supply chain disruptions. However, as energy prices began to stabilize and global inflationary pressures eased in 2023, Malta saw a welcome deceleration in inflation, with headline inflation easing to 4.2% in October 2023. Core inflation, which excludes volatile energy and food prices, also showed signs of moderation, falling to 4.5%. Nonetheless, inflation is projected to remain persistent, staying above the ECB's target of 2% until at least 2025, influenced by tight labor markets, rising wages, and sustained demand pressures.

The fiscal challenges of managing inflation while stimulating growth are formidable, with the government relying heavily on energy subsidies that distort market signals and exacerbate fiscal pressures. A careful policy mix will be required to rein in inflation without stalling economic activity.

Labor Market Dynamics Malta's labor market remains one of the most robust in Europe, with unemployment hovering at near historical lows of 2.5% in 2023. This stability has been buoyed by a steady influx of foreign workers, a critical factor given the country's aging population and low natural labor force growth. The rapid growth of employment—up 5% year-on-year in the first half of 2023—has helped offset the challenges posed by skill shortages and an increasingly tight labor market. Sectors such as remote gaming, ICT, and professional services have been central to this labor market expansion.

However, this dynamic is not without its challenges. Despite relatively low unemployment, significant mismatches remain between the skills required by the market and those available in the local labor force. High demand in sectors like ICT, finance, and gaming contrasts with a lag in educational outcomes and vocational training, leading to skill shortages that could hamper productivity growth. Furthermore, the country's capacity to continue absorbing an expanding workforce will be tested by rising pressure on infrastructure and public services, particularly in housing, health, and education.

Fiscal Policy: Navigating Deficits and Debt for Long-Term Stability

Debt and Deficit Dynamics Malta's fiscal policy remains firmly in expansionary territory, as the government continues to grapple with the aftermath of the pandemic and the ongoing effects of global energy shocks. The fiscal deficit in 2023 is expected to narrow slightly to 4.8% of GDP, but the country's public debt trajectory remains a concern. After rising from 40% of GDP in 2019 to over 52% in 2022, public debt is projected to increase further, reaching 54.5% in 2024. While this remains manageable within the context of Malta's strong domestic financial sector, the country faces significant risks associated with external factors, including energy price volatility and the increasing burden of aging-related costs.

There is a clear need for accelerated fiscal consolidation to reduce these deficits and build fiscal buffers, particularly as Malta faces mounting spending pressures related to aging demographics, healthcare, and infrastructure investments. However, given Malta's small size and limited fiscal space, this will require a careful balancing act to avoid stifling growth while also ensuring long-term fiscal sustainability.

Tax Reforms and Revenue Strategies Malta's tax system is in the midst of a significant transformation, driven in part by the EU's adoption of the Minimum Tax Directive (Pillar II), which aims to level the playing field for multinational enterprises by imposing a minimum corporate tax rate of 15%. Malta's current system, which includes a refundable tax mechanism reducing the effective tax rate for multinational enterprises to just 5%, is no longer sustainable in its current form. As a result, it is recommended that Malta introduce a phased reform of both its corporate income tax and personal income tax systems to ensure long-term competitiveness and revenue stability.

Key to this reform is the gradual phasing out of the tax refund system, which could result in a higher effective tax rate for some multinational enterprises, alongside reductions in the statutory corporate tax rate for domestic firms. The government has been encouraged to introduce a roadmap for these reforms, with a particular focus on aligning the taxation of multinational and domestic enterprises to avoid distortions and maintain investor confidence.

Additionally, the government has been urged to enhance its revenue administration through continued modernization of the Malta Tax and Customs Administration (MTCA). This is critical in boosting tax compliance and reducing the informal economy, which would ultimately support sustainable public finances.

Energy Subsidy Reforms One of the most pressing fiscal reforms is the gradual reduction of energy subsidies, which have placed an immense strain on public finances. Energy subsidies account for a significant portion of Malta's fiscal deficit, at roughly 1.7% of GDP in 2023. While these subsidies have helped shield households from the impact of rising energy costs, they also distort market prices and disincentivize energy conservation and the transition to renewable energy sources.

An exit strategy for these subsidies is recommended, which would involve a gradual transition to market-based pricing for energy while providing targeted support for vulnerable households and businesses. The government is encouraged to adopt a progressive electricity tariff structure, which would provide affordable energy to low-income households while applying cost-recovery pricing to higher levels of consumption.

Investment Landscape: Opportunities in the Green and Digital Transitions

Green Economy Transition Malta is well-positioned to capitalize on its growing commitment to sustainability and the green transition. As a small island economy with limited natural resources, Malta faces unique challenges in energy security and environmental sustainability. However, the government has prioritized the development of renewable energy infrastructure, particularly offshore wind farms and the construction of a second interconnector with Italy, which will help diversify the country's energy sources and reduce its reliance on imported fossil fuels.

The green transition presents substantial investment opportunities, particularly in renewable energy projects, energy-efficient buildings, and waste management. However, Malta's current reliance on fossil fuels for a significant portion of its energy consumption presents an ongoing challenge. The government's ongoing investments in green infrastructure and climate resilience—alongside its commitments under the EU's climate agenda—offer ample opportunities for both domestic and foreign investors.

Digital Transformation The digitalization of Malta's economy is another key growth area, with investments in ICT, innovation, and digital infrastructure poised to drive future growth. Malta has a thriving ICT sector, with a strong focus on blockchain technology, remote gaming, and digital finance. The government's Smart Specialization Strategy, which targets innovation in areas such as health, manufacturing, and digitalization, will play a pivotal role in attracting investment to these high-value sectors. However, there is a need for further investments in research and development (R&D), venture capital, and business process innovation to ensure that Malta remains competitive in the digital economy.

Efforts to address skill shortages in the digital sector through targeted education and training programs will also be crucial in fostering a competitive workforce capable of supporting Malta's growing digital economy.

Real Estate and Housing Malta's real estate market, after a sharp post-pandemic boom, has shown signs of moderation, with residential property prices slowing and the price-to-income ratio beginning to align more closely with

311

market fundamentals. However, housing remains a critical issue, with demand continuing to outstrip supply in many areas, particularly in the rental market. Rising property prices and the high cost of living present a challenge for both locals and migrants, with affordability becoming an increasingly pressing concern.

Government measures, including expanded public housing projects and incentives for first-time buyers, aim to address these challenges. However, longer-term solutions must focus on increasing the supply of housing, improving urban planning, and streamlining the permitting process to meet growing demand.

Strategic Challenges and Opportunities

Structural Reforms Malta's economic future hinges on its ability to implement meaningful structural reforms across various sectors. Boosting productivity will be essential to ensure that growth remains inclusive and sustainable. Key areas for reform include improving education outcomes, enhancing the efficiency of public services, and addressing infrastructure bottlenecks that could constrain future growth.

Further investments in human capital through upskilling and reskilling programs are necessary to match the demands of a rapidly evolving job market. The ongoing efforts to enhance the education system, with a focus on addressing disparities in outcomes for immigrant students, will be vital in securing a future-ready workforce.

Financial Sector Resilience While Malta's financial system is robust, vigilance is needed to monitor risks associated with rising mortgage debt and corporate leverage. Banks are well-capitalized, with high liquidity buffers, but exposure to the real estate sector remains a key risk. The introduction of a sectoral systemic risk buffer (sSyRB) for its banking system in 2023, in collaboration between the Central Bank of Malta and the Malta Financial Services Authority, of 1.5% on residential mortgage exposures. This measure aimed to enhance the resilience of banks against potential housing market shocks, however, it is recommended the authorities consider raising the sSyRB rate and broadening its scope beyond residential mortgages, given banks' increasing and significant exposures to real estate.

However, further monitoring of property market developments, coupled with enhanced stress-testing and macroprudential measures, will be essential to ensure the continued stability of the financial system.

Conclusion: A Path Toward Sustainable, Inclusive, and Resilient Growth

Malta's economic outlook is one of cautious optimism. The country's strong growth trajectory, supported by fiscal discipline and strategic investments in green and digital technologies, offers significant opportunities for both local and international investors. However, the nation must address pressing fiscal challenges, including the need for energy subsidy reforms, tax system modernization, and structural adjustments to ensure long-term economic sustainability. Through continued investment in innovation, education, and infrastructure, Malta can overcome its current challenges and pave the way for a future of resilient, inclusive, and sustainable growth.

References

- IMF Country Report No. 24/229
- IMF Country Report No. 24/216
- IMF Country Report No. 24/240
- IMF Country Report No. 24/152
- IMF Country Report No. 24/85
- IMF Country Report No. 23/189
- IMF Country Report No. 23/386
- IMF Country Report No. 24/70
- IMF Country Report No. 23/411
- IMF Country Report No. 24/107
- IMF Country Report No. 24/292
- IMF Country Report No. 23/395
- IMF Country Report No. 24/28
- IMF Country Report No. 24/72
- IMF Country Report No. 24/308
- IMF Country Report No. 24/23
- IMF Country Report No. 24/268
- IMF Country Report No. 24/75
- IMF Country Report No. 24/163
- IMF Country Report No. 24/155
- IMF Country Report No. 24/246
- IMF Country Report No. 24/242
- IMF Country Report No. 24/120
- IMF Country Report No. 24/285

- IMF Country Report No. 24/177
- IMF Country Report No. 24/137
- IMF Country Report No. 24/33